CONFRONTING SAFFRON DEMOGRAHY

CONFRONTING SAFFRON DEMOGRAPHY

Religion, Fertility, and Women's Status in India

Patricia Jeffery and **Roger Jeffery**

First Edition January 2006

copyright©Three Essays, 2006
All rights reserved

ISBN   978-81-88789-40-5

Three Essays
COLLECTIVE

B-957 Palam Vihar, GURGAON 122 017 India
Phone: 0 9868126587, 0 98683 44843
threeessays@gmail.com
Printed at Glorious Printers, New Delhi

CONTENTS

Acknowledgements

Our research in Bijnor was funded by the Economic and Social Research Council in 1982-3 and 1985 (grant numbers G00230027 and G00232238), by the Overseas Development Administration in 1990-1, by the Economic and Social Research Council again from 2000-2003 (with Craig Jeffrey, grant number R000238495) and by the Wellcome Trust in 2002-5 (grant number GR067231). None of these bears any responsibility for what we have written here.

We are exceptionally grateful to our research assistants over the years, Swaleha Begum, Zarin Rais, the late Radha Rani Sharma, Chhaya Sharma, Shaila Rais, and Manjula Sharma: all of them have gone beyond what we could reasonably ask from assistants and translators. We also want to thank the people of Dharmnagri, Jhakri, Qaziwala and Nangal for their forbearance and good humour in explaining things that seemed obvious to them but which we found it hard to understand.

Earlier versions of Chapter 1 were presented at meetings in Edinburgh (1995), Heidelberg (1996) and Cambridge (2000) and we thank colleagues there and elsewhere for their comments, especially Michael Anderson, Paola Bacchetta, Alaka Basu, Pradip Datta, Christophe Jaffrelot, Donald MacKenzie, Mark Nichter, and Pravin Visaria. The chapter was originally published in 2002 as 'A Population out of Control? Myths about

Muslim Fertility in Contemporary India', *World Development* 30, 11: 1805-1822; a revised version appeared in 2002 as 'We Five, Our Twenty Five: Myths of Population out of Control in Contemporary India', pp.172-199 in Mark Nichter and Margaret Lock (eds): *New Horizons in Medical Anthropology* (London and New York: Routledge, pp. 172-199).

Chapter 2 was originally published in 2001 as 'A Uniform Customary Code? Marital breakdown and women's economic entitlements in western UP', *Contributions to Indian Sociology,* 35, 1: 1-32. Revised versions were published in 2003 in Roger Jeffery and Jens Lerche (eds): *Social and Political Change in Uttar Pradesh: European Perspectives* (New Delhi: Manohar, pp. 77-101) and in Imtiaz Ahmad (ed.): *Divorce and Remarriage among Muslims in India* (New Delhi: Manohar, pp. 101-136). We are grateful to Jens Lerche, Patricia Uberoi and colleagues in Amsterdam, Edinburgh, Kuala Lumpur, Oxford and Prague for comments on earlier versions of this paper.

Chapter 3 was originally presented as 'Engendering Communalism: Everyday and Institutional Aspects of Gender and Community in Bijnor' to a workshop entitled 'Appropriating Gender: Women's Activism and the Politicization of Religion in South Asia' at the Bellagio Study and Conference Center, 1994. Part of this paper was later published in 1999 as 'Gender, Community and the Local State in Bijnor, India' in Patricia Jeffery and Amrita Basu (eds), *Resisting the Sacred and the Secular: Women's Activism and Politicized Religion in South Asia* (New Delhi: Kali for Women, pp.123-141). The other part was presented at a conference in the School of Oriental and African Studies and published in 2000 as 'Identifying Differences: Gender Politics and Community in Rural Bijnor, UP', in Julia Leslie and Mary McGee (eds) *Gender Constructs in Indian Religion and Society* (Delhi: Oxford University Press, pp.286-309). These two papers have been re-combined and updated here in the light of the research we carried out in Bijnor in 2000-2 with Craig Jeffrey on education, and in 2002-5 on health.

Patricia Jeffery

Edinburgh, August 2005   Roger Jeffery

Saffron Demography and the Common Wisdom

Saffron demography' rests on claims that there are essential differences between Hindu and Muslim population dynamics in India. The central tenets comprise a set of pernicious myths that have been repeated so often, and with so much authority by right-wing Hindu politicians, that they have become part of a 'common wisdom'. Saffron demography is primarily concerned with the relationships between religion (on the one hand) and fertility and population growth (on the other). Inter-religious differences in mortality, for instance, are rarely mentioned, and migration is mentioned only to highlight the possible effects of illegal immigration, not the full range of migration flows within and beyond India's boundaries. In part, this fixation reflects how the 'overpopulation discourse' is "the most important mobilisation of 'population' as an object of knowledge for governance in modern India" (Hodges 2004: 1163). But the obsessive concern with Muslim fertility in itself demonstrates the Islamophobic basis for the discussions. Such a focus produces an unbalanced account, one that ignores central and urgent demographic debates in India today that have been conducted with almost no consideration of their differential effects on religious communities – such as the effects of female infanticide or neglect and sex-selective abortions on the juvenile sex ratio (and thus, before long, on the adult sex ratio), or the likely effects of a looming AIDS crisis.

Saffron demographers (though they rarely seem to have formal training in demography) instead focus on changes in the proportions of the population by religious community from one Census to the next, and argue that Hindus face a minority status within some specifiable period in the future. Most professional demographers, however, would argue that long-term projections are fraught with so many unknown variables that it is foolish to take them seriously. Consider only the possibility (much proclaimed but still not taken seriously in India) that an AIDS pandemic is beginning to sweep the country: even the more conservative estimates of the demographic effects of such a catastrophe would change all the predictions based on extrapolating from the current situation.

Writers from the Hindu Right, however, are less concerned with shedding light than with generating heat: scare-mongering is their purpose and their language betrays this goal, as when they talk of 'the Muslim population in India exploding' and 'the Hindu population declining' (Rai n.d.: 16). Such writers are in a long tradition that has assumed that the social and political influence of a population is in direct proportion to its size. As Pradip Datta has shown, they have made exaggerated claims that 'Hindus are Dying' (see also Basu 1996; Datta 1993; Datta 1999) – claims generated in large measure because of the introduction by the British of decennial censuses in which one of the few 'facts' recorded and published was the religious group to which a person belonged (Appadurai 1993; Cohn 1987).

The issue of the growth rates of religious communities gained more public prominence from 2003 onwards as a result of three interlinked events. The first was the publication in July 2003 of a book entitled *Religious Demography of India* (Joshi et al. 2003) that provides a detailed encapsulation of what we have called Saffron Demography. The book attracted publicity because it had a Foreword from the then Home Minister and Deputy Prime Minister, L.K. Advani; because its publication was supported by the Indian Council for Social Science Research (an autonomous body under the Government of India); and because it came from an apparently prestigious institution, the Centre for Policy Studies, Chennai. For many Indians, its main message – that 'the proportion of Indian Religionists [Hindus, Sikhs, Buddhists, Jains, Parsis and Jews] in India is likely to fall below 50 per cent early in the latter half of the twenty-first century' (Joshi et al. 2003: xix) – will probably have come as no surprise and has been accepted uncritically. But its whole basis was fundamentally flawed, as several critics soon pointed out (Bhattacharya 2003; Chatterjee 2003; Dayal 2003; Verghese 2003). Other critics, unfortunately, displayed their own demographic illiteracy (e.g. Chamadia & Gatade 2003), but the main tenor of response in the

English-medium press was unremittingly and accurately hostile.

The most damning criticism came in a withering review in Economic and Political Weekly (Jayaraj & Subramanian 2004). Noting that the Centre for Policy Studies has no track record in demography, and that the authors of *Religious Demography in India* were physicists, Jayaraj and Subramanian take their claims to pieces. Jayaraj and Subramanian point out that 'Indian Religionists' is an obviously incoherent term, whose use is clearly political: to separate out Muslims and Christians, and to accuse them of introducing heterogeneity into the Indian population. They then note that 'India' in *Religious Demography in India* is sometimes defined as the current Republic of India but sometimes as present-day India, Pakistan and Bangladesh. Only in the latter sense could any prediction that 'Indian Religionists' might become a minority be meaningful, since the share of Muslims and Christians in the population of the Republic of India was less than 15 per cent in 1991 and (as the 2001 Census showed when the relevant figures were released in 2004) less than 16 per cent in 2001. Jayaraj and Subramanian then show that the authors' use of statistical regression techniques in Religious Demography in India is inadequate for predictive purposes: using such regression techniques, one could predict that the year by which 'Indian Religionists' would become a minority in 'India' (i.e. including Bangladesh and Pakistan) might be any year between 2065 and 2181 – or never, depending on the equation chosen. In other words, Jayaraj and Subramanian establish that Saffron Demographers cannot produce plausible evidence for their claims that Hindus will be 'outnumbered' by Muslims and Christians.

This debunking did not stop a similar set of prejudices being aired in September 2004 when the Census Commissioner released figures from the 2001 Census. For the first time, published tables showed the relationships between religion and a number of social variables, including juvenile sex ratios (for details see Registrar General & Census Commissioner 2004). The first press release accompanying the report seemingly showed that the total number of Indian Muslims had grown more rapidly in 1991-2001 than it had in 1981-1991. Not until the Census Commissioner released adjusted figures three days later, was it possible to see that the first figures released had compared the 1991 population totals (when two States with relatively large Muslim populations – Assam, and Jammu and Kashmir – could not be enumerated because of the security situation) with 2001 (when both these States were enumerated) (Bose 2005: 370). Comparing like with like – the only professionally and politically responsible approach – showed that the growth rates of all religious groups were declining. Excluding Assam and Jammu and Kashmir from all the calculations, it became clear that the Muslim population had grown by 33 per cent between 1981 and 1991, and by 29 per cent between 1991 and 2001. The equivalent figures for Hindus were 23 per cent between 1981 and 1991, and 20 per cent between 1991 and 2001. Both rates of growth were declining, the Muslim rate was declining slightly faster than that of Hindus, and so the differences between them were also smaller in 1991-2001 than they had been in 1981-1991.

Nevertheless, these figures all show that there is a difference in growth rates: Muslims are (very slowly) growing as a proportion of the population of the Republic of India. In January 2005 the debate on how to understand and explain this difference was taken much further in articles published in a special issue of the foremost Indian social science journal, Economic and Political Weekly (EPW), to which we also contributed (Jeffery & Jeffery 2005). We shall contribute further to this debate on differential demographic behaviour in this volume, and respond (in the Afterword to this volume) to some of the points made there and in a further comment by Mari Bhat (Bhat 2005). First, however, we shall set out some of the wider implications of Saffron Demography and the common wisdom it both supports and draws upon. We then set out our own agenda – our own views of what it means to be Muslim or Hindu in contemporary India, and how demographic analyses can contribute to understanding this. Finally we set out the context of our research, and outline the structure of this volume.

Stereotypes and Stigma

Many Indians, if asked, would say that there are significant differences between members of the Muslim minority and those in the Hindu majority. Our own experience of this comes from repeated discussions in India and elsewhere. In Bijnor, the district in western Uttar Pradesh (UP) where we have carried out most of our research since 1982, we have been readily plied with communalist discourses, often linked to the notion that Bijnor is backward because it has so many Muslims, and specifically mentioning the status of women in Islam. These discourses draw on Islamophobic ideas – ideas that have a long provenance, and can be traced, in Western Europe, to the impacts of the Crusades, the wars against the Moors in 15th Century Spain, and European colonisation of the 18th and 19th centuries – the latter so well analysed by Edward Said (Said 1978). There is almost as long a history within India of anti-Muslim views; and (as in the rest of the world) they seem to be growing rather than declining. There is, then, a common wisdom in India to which many people subscribe – in some measure at least – that tends to essentialise Hindus and Muslims; that ascribes to Muslims anti-nationalist views or behaviour; and that is highly gendered in its implications.

Movements associated with politicised religion – especially the Hindu Right[1] – have often essentialised the terms 'Hindu' and 'Muslim' (Bacchetta 1993; Bacchetta 1994; Basu 1995a; Hasan 1988). To essentialise identities entails assuming that those that are given at birth (gender, nationality, religion) are the only authentic sources of identity. 'Authenticity' is often central in identity politics, yet it rests on deeply problematic assumptions about cultures as internally homogeneous, timeless, and for ever distinguishable from one another (Bhabha 1990; Hall 1991; Hall et al. 1992; Said 1993). For the Hindu Right, essentialising Hindus and Muslims promotes their political agenda because it works to separate Muslims from the rest of Indians and to target them for punitive and hostile actions. In these ways it leads Hindus to focus on a false unity (as Hindus) rather than to recognise their diverse and often conflicting interests on the basis of their other identities, such as caste membership, class, occupation or gender.[2]

The loyalty of Indian Muslims to the Indian nation has often been questioned by the Hindu Right, partly deriving from their resentment over Partition, which is seen as entirely a Muslim responsibility, and reinforced by rumours of Pakistani spies, by comments on Bangladeshi immigrants, and – as we shall spell out in more detail in Chapter 1 – high Muslim fertility. For Saffron Demographers, Muslims pose a threat to the Indian nation, both by making a major contribution to excessive population growth, and because, when their numbers permit it, they will provide Pakistan with the opportunity to invade. These ideas are repeated in media controlled by the Hindu Right, in the actions and comments of members of the judiciary who support the Hindu Right, as well as in political speeches on behalf of the Bharatiya Janata Party (BJP), the main political voice of the Hindu Right. The Hindu Right claims that Muslims are united behind a political agenda – to take over India – and that this is a compelling reason for demanding Hindu unity.

The Hindu Right also argues that, despite their 'anti-national' character, Indian Muslims were 'pampered' and 'appeased' by Congress governments intent on securing their 'Muslim vote bank'. The notion of a 'vote bank' revolves around the somewhat mythical assumption that groups of people, particularly Muslims, vote en bloc in local and national elections because their leaders can deliver their followers' votes. Like the other claims that Indian Muslims share overriding identifications as Muslims, this has little basis in truth. Muslims tended to vote for Congress until the late 1980s, but not uniformly so: sizeable numbers also voted for parties championing the interests of the urban working classes and the rural dispossessed, and this has become more common in recent years. Nonetheless, the notion that Muslims vote en bloc is an important part of the common wisdom, and it carries the clear presumption that such behaviour undermines national unity.

Gender issues – images of male and female citizens – are often prominent in nationalist discourses. High profile politicised religion in India – as elsewhere in the region and beyond – is deeply gendered in its manifestations, whether in the publications and speeches of its ideologues or in the operation of distinctive systems of family law (Anthias & Yuval-Davis 1992; Basu 1995b; Mann 1994; Moghadam 1994a; Moghadam 1994b). Over the past 100 years or so, there has been an increasingly intense discussion about what it means to be a Hindu man, with notions of tolerance and non-violence (associated particularly with the Gandhian approach to Hinduism) giving way to claims about their willingness to defend Hinduism with violence should it be necessary (Pandey 1991; Pandey 1993: 238-72). The Hindu Right has tried to make the God Ram the ideal for Hindu men to follow, and to characterise Ram not as vulnerable, self-doubting or frail, but as aggressively masculine and willing to force doubters and non-believers into submission (Pandey 1993: 15). As a contrast, 'the Hindu woman' is idealised as a respected mother of the nation, expected to rear pure and patriotic Hindu citizens, or to protect the birthplace of Ram with the ferocity of a mother defending her children's interests (Chhachhi 1991; Chhachhi 1994; Mazumdar 1992; Mazumdar 1995; Sarkar 1991; Sarkar & Butalia 1995).

Muslim men are represented as unmitigatedly aggressive: when 'riots' occur, the Hindu Right characterises them as the fault of hot-blooded Muslim men, rather than (as is much more often the case) attacks on Muslims or provocations by Hindus who know that the state apparatus will normally protect them (Brass 2002). But in addition (and with direct relevance for this volume) this aggression is said to have sexual implications. The essentialised 'Muslim woman' is supposedly victimised by Muslim men (who are caricatured as sexually voracious and polygamous), and in need of rescue by gallant and fair-minded Hindu men (Bacchetta 1994; Basu 1995a; Basu 1999; Basu et al. 1993; Hasan 1999; Kapur & Cossman 1995; Sarkar 1993). For instance, the 'vulnerability' of Muslim women was a key issue in the Shah Bano affair (which we discuss in Chapter 2 of this volume) and latterly, but mercifully less dramatically, in relation to the 'triple talåq' (the notion that a Muslim man can divorce his wife at will). Although the provisions of Muslim and Hindu Family Law alike are discriminatory on grounds of sex, portrayals of the Muslim woman as oppressed by Islamic doctrine, seclusion practices and so forth have taken root in public discourse (Kapur & Cossman 1995; Kishwar 1986; Parashar 1992). The common wisdom, then, is that Muslims have more children than members of other religious groups because Muslim women are more backward, more constrained by religion and more closely controlled by their menfolk. Compared to Hindu men, Muslim men have more children because they can take more than one wife, they can divorce more easily, and they more readily follow the wishes of their religious leaders, whose desire is for Muslims to outnumber Hindus in order to take political power. Thus purdah, polygamy, educational backwardness, women's status and a political agenda are all rolled together to 'explain' fertility among Muslims.

The common wisdom thus portrays Muslims and Hindus as essentially different and Muslims as a threat to the Indian Nation. Women and population issues are entwined into an enduring image: the Muslim woman's victimhood and backwardness are said to be major reasons for her supposed high fertility. This picture is, however, highly misleading. The common wisdom is heavily influenced by pernicious stereotypes peddled by members of the Hindu Right, who have exaggerated the size and stability of fertility differentials, and created untenable explanations for their false claims. Our position, as set out in the main chapters of this volume, rests on very different ideas about identity, religion and demographic change.

Our Agenda

As against those (such as the Hindu Right, but also conservative Muslim leaders) who see communal identities as fixed and central to how people see themselves, we argue that all social identities are fluid, and that boundaries between competing groupings are specific to particular times and places (Jenkins 1996). Communal identities are negotiated and socially constructed rather than 'natural or 'essential', and communal boundaries and their markers are permeable and fluid rather than static, and continually sustained and re-worked through social praxis (Barth 1969). Distinctions made by locals often seem small-scale and even trivial to an outsider, but if they are compelling – though not entirely stable – markers of difference to people on the ground, they can have immense social and political significance.

In other words, claims about fundamental loyalties must be continually re-asserted if they are to withstand challenges from cross-cutting and competing sources of identity (gender, class, caste) or countervailing tendencies that stress people's common humanity. For instance, we have seen how the significance of communal identities has changed in Bijnor. In the early 1980s, communal identities existed alongside other sources of identification – aside from gender – that were also struggling to be heard. Sometimes, too, countervailing voices claimed a common humanity with a common origin and destination, beside which mere matters of ritual and custom (rðt, riwåj) and of Hindu and Muslim are of negligible importance. For instance, during the rioting in Bijnor town in October 1990, local Hindu and Muslim politicians called a large public meeting in which leaders from all the surrounding villages made speeches in favour of communal harmony, and stressed the common humanity of all, whatever their caste or religious allegiance. Although this strategy succeeded in reducing tension, and no violence took place in these villages, most people we talked to after the meeting were cynical about the speakers' underlying motives. We also heard rhetorics stressing a common humanity when people wanted to smooth over our persistence in visiting all manner of homes in the villages. Thus during weddings, Roger was sometimes introduced to other guests – in apparently glowing terms – with reference to his insistence on regarding people as insån (human) rather than as Hindu or Muslim. Such rhetorics sometimes had a rather trite feel to them, however, and seemed to carry little weight in local political discourse.

The most obvious ways in which the term 'Hindu' has been challenged in recent times has been in whether the Scheduled Castes (SCs) and Other Backward Classes (OBCs) have been willing to accept the Hindu Right's attempt to develop an all-encompassing Hindu unity against Muslims.[3] In the period around 1990, for example, the distinctions between OBCs, SCs and other Hindus acquired a particularly heightened political salience because of the government's plan to implement the Mandal Commission's recommendations to extend the reservation of college places and government jobs (Beteille 1992; Engineer 1991b; Jeffery & Jeffery 1997). Jats in Bijnor argued that reservations gave SCs and OBCs an unfair advantage in education and employment vis-à-vis the 'forward castes'.[4] Muslims also resented the reservations, on the grounds that they themselves were just as deserving as the SCs and OBCs, and just as excluded from the economic mainstream. Around the same time, the then Chief Minister of UP, Mulayam Singh Yadav of the Samajwadi Party (SP), held rallies throughout UP, trying to mobilise OBCs, SCs and Muslims around issues of class and caste domination. Moreover, many members of the 'little' or lower castes (*chhote zat*) distanced themselves from the dominant Hindu castes. Like the SCs and OBCs, they often asserted that Jats and other big land-holding groups treated SCs and little castes badly. They argued that it would be a mistake to be hoodwinked into believing they had interests in common with those who dominated them in everyday life. But some groups among the SCs would not accept the Bahujan Samaj Party's (BSP) claims that it was acting in the interests of all SCs, asserting instead that it really represented only Chamars. In rural Bijnor, Muslims and Chamars (also known as Jatavs, and the largest Scheduled Caste) were generally mutually disdainful, so it is not clear that alliances such as those being attempted by Mulayam Singh Yadav or (at times) by the BSP, would be any more successful than an alliance between the BJP and either the BSP or the SP.

Economic differences (or perceptions of conflicting economic interests) sometimes constitute an important element in communal politics. But they do not necessarily do so in a straightforward way and almost certainly cannot alone suffice to 'explain' communal disturbances and tensions. Thus we also distance ourselves from those who think that communal (or caste) differences can be explained in any simple way by conflicting economic interests: contrasts between the situations in western UP and in eastern UP, for example, cannot be explained just in terms of different patterns of landholding or employment opportunities (Lerche 2003).

In sum, then, Bijnor's rural society is shot through with cross-cutting fracture lines, sometimes papered over and muted, sometimes coming dramatically into the foreground. 'Hindu' and 'Muslim' are temporary and partial categories, sometimes relevant to people's behaviour, sometimes irrelevant, sometimes internally fragmented, sometimes providing clear bases for action. People's identifications are socially constructed in the face of competing alternatives, and reflect the outcomes of political struggles to win people's loyalties, whether rallying imagined communities of believers or of those subject to class or caste oppression. A sense of commonality – and a sense of difference from the Other – does not arise naturally or reflect natural or primordial allegiances. Other imagined communities – regional, class, gender or occupational – can be fabricated and may carry greater conviction. As such, we should not expect people's identifications to be carved in stone, or their loyalties to have finality and stability.

Consequently, in our work we have highlighted the falsity and perniciousness of negative stereotypes of Muslims that rely on reified and rigidified contrasts on the basis of religion, and ignore the parallels and similarities between Hindus and Muslims, for example in domestic and gender politics (Jeffery & Jeffery 1996a; Jeffery et al. 1989).[5] Taking the particular case of demography, our general argument goes as follows:

1. That there are differences in demographic behaviour between Muslims and Hindus that remain after taking account of their different social locations;

2. That the differences in fertility that are the major focus of debate (and therefore of our response) are not, however, sufficient to lead to substantial changes in the balance between different religious categories in India within the foreseeable future;

3. That these differences, moreover, are not a result of conscious efforts by Muslims to increase their fertility, but are largely attributable to Muslims' minority position and marginalisation; and

4. That focussing on differences between Muslims and Hindus tends – in very deleterious ways – to draw attention away from the problems that poor people (and especially women) face as a result of the failures of the UP state.

We start from the position that, in the Bijnor countryside as elsewhere, there are no direct relationships between fertility (and mortality) and people's differing social and economic locations. Rather, these relationships are mediated by how people themselves make sense of the world around them and imagine futures for themselves and their families. As a result, broad-brush accounts, ones that rely heavily on large-scale or national surveys and/or on the Census, are by themselves inadequate (see also Bose 2005: 374). Special surveys are, of course, valuable sources. But they share some weaknesses. In general, the larger the population surveyed, the less reliance can be placed on the validity of the research results. Census enumerators may ask, for example, about who is alive now, and who has been born in one or two previous years. The other variables considered (such as the presence or absence of health facilities, or the relationships between a woman's schooling and how many living children she has) are analysed in part because they are available, and not necessarily because they are the most important variables. Large-scale surveys also have to depend on many – often ill-motivated – assistants, who are tempted to take short-cuts rather than concern themselves with data quality. Moreover, the analysis of large-scale surveys must inevitably abstract from real individuals and the relationships within which they are embedded, and instead focus on relationships between variables (such as the education of the mother and the number of children she has had). Unfortunately, few Indian demographers, economists or sociologists have gone beyond demographic data gathering through large-scale sample surveys (Bose 2003). Many mainstream Indian demographers do not acknowledge the weaknesses of their favoured, survey methodology and pour scorn on small-scale studies (see, e.g. Reddy 2003).Yet small-scale studies can contextualise what people say and why they say it, because data quality is a central concern and people can be asked a much wider range of questions, with repeated visits if necessary. We need to find ways of combining large-scale surveys (where the numbers are sufficient to permit the isolation of the impact of multiple variables, and conclusions may be seen as sufficiently robust to inform policy) with case studies (which can provide explanations of behaviour that are much more persuasive).[6]

The Context of Our Research: UP and Bijnor District

In a classic article, Dyson and Moore characterised a 'northern demographic regime' in India as follows. Fertility rates and child mortality rates are high by Indian standards; rates of contraceptive use are low; there are high levels of maternal mortality; and there are extremely masculine sex ratios. These sex ratios are mainly a result of levels of female child mortality that are much higher than those of males, reflecting the 'son preferences' associated with parental anxieties about providing dowries for daughters and having sons to ensure support in old age (Dyson & Moore 1983). These demographic and social features are typical of Uttar Pradesh (UP) as a whole. UP is India's most populous State, with about 16 per cent of India's population. According to the 2001 Census (Registrar General & Census Commissioner 2002), UP is less urban than the rest of India; it has a more masculine sex ratio (at 898 women for every 1000 men compared to an all-India figure of 933); and it has more children (nearly 20 per cent of India's children aged under 6 live in UP).

Dyson and Moore linked this northern demographic regime to aspects of kinship, residence and property ownership, marriage arrangement and gender politics that we shall outline in more detail in Chapter 2. For the moment, we merely note that young married women living in the northern demographic regime generally have a very limited capacity for self-determination. Young women lack social power in their own right because they nearly always migrate away from their natal kin on marriage, to the villages of their husband and his family. They are severely constrained by their lack of economic independence and by other aspects of their domestic circumstances – for instance, in respect of making decisions about their fertility and about health care for themselves and other family members, such as small children (Jeffery & Jeffery 1996a: 1-37).

About a quarter of Indian Muslims live in UP, where there were over thirty million (or just under 18.5 per cent of the State's total population) in 2001. Less than two thirds (64 per cent) live in the rural areas, compared with the overall UP figure of just under 80 per cent. Several studies indicate that Muslims in UP are under-represented among the more affluent sectors and over-represented amongst the poor. In UP, rural Muslims have an average monthly expenditure per person that is 97 per cent of that of Hindus, but in urban areas, Muslim expenditures are only 73 per cent of those of urban Hindus (John & Mutatkar 2005: 1341). Muslim town-dwellers tend to inhabit particular residential areas and are especially associated with artisanal activities such as weaving and metal work; rural Muslims are generally middle or poor peasants, landless agricultural labourers or semi-skilled labourers (mechanics, weavers, etc.). According to the 2001 Census, only 38 per cent of Muslims over the age of 6 are literate, compared to 46 per cent in UP as a whole (see also Shariff 1995). When class is held constant, however, the similar domestic arrangements, property rights, linguistic patterns and diet of north Indian Muslims and Hindus, and the distinctively South Asian flavour to Islam, are striking (Ahmad 1973; Ahmad 1976; Ahmad 1981; Hasan 1991; Hasan 1997; Mann 1992).

Bijnor District is one of UP's north-western districts, located to the east of the River Ganges as it emerges from the Himalayan foothills, about 150 km north east of Delhi. In Indian terms, the area is not poor. In terms of economic indicators, Bijnor was in the top 14 of the 63 districts in UP in 2000 (Singh 2001: Table VIII.8). The Bijnor countryside is flat and intensively cultivated, and has benefited from assured water supplies since 1965, mainly using private tube-well irrigation. Improved varieties of sugarcane, wheat and rice are the overwhelmingly dominant crops. The district has had a less skewed pattern of landholding than many other parts of UP, although about 20 per cent of the households in our research villages are landless, and another 40 per cent do not have enough land for subsistence. The district is less affluent, though, than districts to the west of the Ganges (Meerut, Muzaffarnagar, Saharanpur) that have had canal irrigation since the end of the nineteenth century. Further, there is little large-scale manufacturing industry in the main towns of Bijnor district – apart from sugar processing – and there has been nothing comparable to the extensive ribbon development of industrial activities in the Delhi-Ghaziabad-Meerut-Muzaffarnagar corridor between the Ganges and the Jumna. Nevertheless, the completion of the Madhya Ganga Barrage across the Ganges near Bijnor town in the mid 1980s enhanced trading and communication opportunities to the west of Bijnor, and Delhi, Meerut and Muzaffarnagar are now easily accessible by bus. On most criteria of social and economic development, Bijnor District is rather more 'developed' than the districts of central or eastern UP.

Its social indicators, however, are much lower than would be expected from its economic ranking. In regard to educational infrastructure, for instance, Bijnor ranked 57th of the 63 districts in UP, a state with one of the poorest showings in India (Singh 2001: Table VIII.3). Adult literacy rates in UP as a whole (43 per cent of women and 70 per cent of men) are lower than the all India rates (54 per cent of women and 76 per cent of men). According to 2001 Census data (Registrar General & Census Commissioner 2002), Bijnor District literacy rates for females aged 7 or above were slightly better than the UP figures, at 47 per cent, while those for men were almost exactly the same as those for UP as a whole.

Bijnor district has a relatively large Muslim population. Overall, in 2001 about 42 per cent of the population was Muslim, 35 per cent was caste Hindu and 21 per cent was

Scheduled Caste, with the rest Sikhs and small numbers of Christians and Buddhists. As in several other districts in western UP, the towns of Bijnor District have a Muslim majority, with 67 per cent of the urban population in 2001, although the new suburbs of the bigger towns – which are not necessarily defined as 'urban' for census purposes – are often dominated by Hindus. Unusually, however, the district has a relatively large proportion of rural Muslims – about 34 per cent in 2001 (Registrar General & Census Commissioner 2002). Some villages in Bijnor District are dominated by particular Hindu castes and others have no substantial settlements of Muslims, many have evenly balanced Hindu and Muslim populations and yet others are exclusively or largely Muslim. There are distinctive and separate Muslim institutions and class and caste structures, to a greater degree than in areas where Muslims are few in number. Bijnor Muslims, then, are diverse and located in a range of class positions, from (mainly small) landowners and businessmen to landless labourers, from cattle traders to barbers and midwives. This diversity was central to our decision to base our initial research on childbearing in the district, because there are few ethnographies of areas in India where large numbers of Muslims live.

Muslims, however, are much weaker politically than their numbers in Bijnor would suggest. Brahmans dominate trade and commerce, while Jats and Rajputs dominate agriculture and small-scale rural industries (like sugar production). The Scheduled Castes have access to several government schemes and also benefit locally because Bijnor is a 'reserved constituency' (restricted to Scheduled Caste candidates) in national elections. Mayavati, a leader of the BSP, represented the seat in the 1980s. In the 1991 elections the parliamentary constituency was won by the BJP, who retained it in 1996 and 1998, but lost it to the combined candidate of the SP and Rashtriya Lok Dal in 2004. In the elections for the UP State Assembly, after a clean sweep of all seven Bijnor seats in 1991, the BJP lost ground to other parties: in 2002 the BJP held only 3 seats, with two going to the SP and one each to the BSP and the Communist Party of India.

Members of Parliament and of the UP State Assembly can be very important channels of resources: having a link to a successful politician can make a major difference to one's chances of getting or keeping a job, a scholarship, or admission to public facilities like hospitals. Politicians are also symbols for the communities they come from, and their public actions affect the everyday perceptions and influence of ordinary people of their own and other communities. We discuss everyday communalism in Chapter 3 of this volume: here we merely want to point out that it is not just a question of the numbers of Hindus and Muslims living in the area, but also their differential placing in structures of power and influence in the area and how they engage in stereotyping one another.

Some of this stereotyping is directly relevant to the concerns of this volume, in particular those relating to women. In common with most stereotypes, however, close scrutiny reveals a more complex situation. For example (as we explore more fully in Chapter 2) contrary to common stereotypes of the restricted Muslim woman, in some ways a typical Muslim woman seems rather better placed than the typical Hindu woman in rural Bijnor. Thus, while son preferences are expressed irrespective of religious community, maternity history and census data from our study villages indicate that sex ratios are markedly less masculine among Muslims than among Hindus (Jeffery & Jeffery 1997: 68, 230-35). Census data from 2001 and other sources support the argument that 'girls in India may be least at risk with Muslim parents, and most at risk with parents who are caste Hindus' (Borooah & Iyer 2005: 419, emphasis in the original). In some measure, the pressure to provide dowries helps to create the more masculine sex ratios of surviving children among Hindus: Muslims less often report dowry demands and dowry harassment of young married women than local Hindus do, and Muslim dowries do not include cash. Furthermore, since Muslims generally arrange their children's marriages within a small geographical radius (about 3 km or less, and occasionally even within the village) and/or with people who are already closely related, married Muslim women are normally less cut off from their natal kin than are Hindu women. Yet such differences do not appear to translate into greater access to education, health care, or contraception for most Muslim women; and in the Bijnor populations we have studied, Muslim women generally experience somewhat higher levels of fertility and child deaths (though not necessarily higher than low caste and poor Hindu women), largely due to their concentration in the lower levels of the economic hierarchy (Jeffery & Jeffery 1998; Jeffery et al. 1989; Jeffery & Jeffery 1997). We discuss the reasons for this in more detail in Chapter 3.

In the rest of this volume we draw heavily on our research in four Bijnor villages, and in the district headquarters, Bijnor town, and we want here to convey something of that experience, and some basic information about the villages, as a backdrop to what follows. Our earliest memories of rural Bijnor are of careering along in a UP Roadways bus at dusk, almost overwhelmed by the heady vapours from the numerous sugar factories processing the sugarcane that is the major cash crop in the area. That was in February 1982. Within a few weeks, the District Medical Officer had given us permission to live in the disused operating theatre of the Dharmnagri dispensary, where we lived until the spring of 1983.

In that research we tried to collect data on child-bearing and issues of maternal and child health, through involving ourselves as fully as we could in the everyday lives of two villages some five minutes walk away from one another (Jhakri and Dharmnagri). In 1982 Jhakri had an exclusively Muslim population of 309 (712 in 2003), about 75 per cent Sheikh, plus 11 households of Telis and 12 of Julahas. Dharmnagri had a population in 1982 of 586 (1,325 in 2003), comprised of caste Hindus (71 households of Sahnis, 28 of Dhimars, nine of Jats, seven of Rajputs, and the remaining 19 made up of small numbers of other castes) and Scheduled Castes (71 households of Chamars, sometimes also known as Jatavs, and three of Balmikis). In this research and in a two-month follow-up visit in 1985 we selected equal numbers of Hindu and Muslim 'key informants', 40 couples from a range of class and caste positions, in which the wife had recently given birth or was pregnant (for more details, see Jeffery et al. 1989: 233-7).

In July 1990, we returned to live in the same dispensary, living there for a year while we carried out research mostly in two further villages – Nangal and Qaziwala – on aspects of social demography and caste cultures. In 1990, Nangal had a population of about 4,250 (5,250 in 2001), nearly half Chamars, 25 per cent Jats, about 12 per cent Muslims and the rest from a variety of small Hindu castes. In 1991, Qaziwala had a population of about 2,650 (3,500 in 2001), almost all Muslims, of whom about 60 per cent were Sheikhs, 25 per cent were Qasais, and the rest small Muslim castes, with only 3 per cent SCs and Hindus. In Nangal and Qaziwala we selected 40 additional key informant couples with the wife aged between 25 and 35, covering a range of educational experiences and marriage distances, again equally divided between Hindus and Muslims (for more details, see Jeffery & Jeffery 1997). We also spent time with Dharmnagri and Jhakri villagers, finding out what had happened since our previous research, conducting another household census, and discussing current news – especially the violence that engulfed Bijnor town in October-December 1990.

In 2000-02, we spent two eight-month periods living in Bijnor town, carrying out research in secondary schools in and around all these four villages, but focusing again on Nangal and Qaziwala. This was the first occasion in which we were explicitly interested in the resources Bijnor town offered or controlled, such as secondary schooling, but again we talked to people in Dharmnagri and Jhakri when we had the opportunity. In 2002-04, Patricia again spent long periods in Jhakri and Dharmnagri carrying out a study of the continuities and changes in demography and health, especially maternal and child health, and following up the original key informants and their families.

In the course of our research in the area, then, we have collected general economic and demographic data about these four villages from local men and women, and have interviewed numerous staff in schools and health facilities. We have also conducted semi-structured interviews with almost 100 women, visiting most of them many times over this 20-year period. Most of the women were born and raised in other villages in the District. Thus, although the material presented here primarily pertains to the four research villages, our arguments are supplemented with information about many other villages in the locality.

Structure of the Book

Chapter 1 describes and criticises myths propagated by Hindu nationalist organisations about the scale and causes of fertility differentials between Hindus and Muslims in India. We challenge these views – views that we suggested above are part of a common wisdom about demographic patterns in India – by examining how demographers have addressed the role of religion in fertility differences, along with other factors that affect fertility, such as class, caste, education, region and urban/rural residence. We further suggest that elaborate statistical analyses of large-scale data sets are not readily sensitive to local-level variations and we use our micro-level research findings to illuminate both Hindu Right political rhetoric and the limitations of macro-level demographic analyses. If significant differences between Muslim and Hindu fertility rates remain after taking regional differences, variations in socio-economic position, and occupation into consideration, then these have more to do with the effect of Muslims' position as an excluded minority than the effects of theological doctrines.

Chapter 2 takes this argument one step further by focusing on aspects of everyday gender politics in western UP, particularly on women's entitlements to economic support after marital breakdown. First, the crucial parallels in the everyday domestic lives of Hindu and Muslim women in rural Bijnor, combined with case material on marital breakdown, undermine Hindu Right assertions that Muslim women are uniquely oppressed by their menfolk and victimised by Islam. Second, political developments on the national stage – the Shah Bano case and the controversy over the Muslim Women (Protection of Rights on Divorce) Act of 1986, the Babari Masjid campaign, and the associated communalisation of politics – were highly significant in terms of local-level communal politics in Bijnor (Basu 1995c; Jeffery & Jeffery 1994). Yet the implications for local-level gender politics are less clear. Contrary to Hindu activists' assumptions, there is no evidence that the Muslim Women Act privileges Muslim men vis-à-vis Hindu men by enabling them to avoid making maintenance payments to their ex-wives. Indeed, the Act has had no impact on the economic situations of ordinary Muslim women in rural Bijnor: they are left in essentially the same kind of plight following marital breakdown as their Hindu neighbours from similar class backgrounds – just as they had been before the legislation. This chapter, then, shows that everyday gender politics – the lived realities of Muslim and Hindu women in western UP – has relatively little to do either with formal law or with theology. Bringing local-level gender politics – a 'uniform customary code' –

into the frame alongside the communa-lisation of politics raises serious questions about the efficacy of the law in protecting women's rights. It also highlights dilemmas for feminist activists in regard to their strategic priorities and the potential for mobilising rural women around the struggle for gender equity.

These considerations are addressed in more detail in Chapter 3, where we focus on the social and political significance of 'religious' community membership. We argue that Muslim women – as members of a religious minority – are more adversely affected than Hindu women by commu-nalised social and political processes that operate at the local level but beyond the domestic arena. Women from different religious groups themselves debate many common aspects of their situations, but rarely come together across the communal divide. Muslim women have few allies in their attempts to combat sexism in their domestic circumstances and gendered communalism outside. We show how the interactions between national politics and events have had an impact on the local perceptions of Muslims and Hindus, and how we need to understand both the impact of significant events (such as the riots in Bijnor in 1990, or in Gujarat in 2002) and how the state affects life in everyday ways. In UP, the government has faced severe financial constraints since 1991. Educational and health facilities (already very limited) have deteriorated still further – and Muslim women have been disproportionately affected by these changes. Our research suggests that, in combination, the communalised nature of these services, and their increasingly limited reach, have left Muslim women more at the mercy of the market than Hindu or SC women from comparable class backgrounds. It is ironic, therefore, that Muslims in general are blamed for their fertility and backwardness. The political and economic marginalisation of which they are more likely to be victims is a crucial element in their educational trajectories and in their reproductive health and contraceptive decision-making. Finally, in the Afterword, we consider the more recent debates on the issue.

Notes

[1]   The 'Hindu Right' comprises several organisations also known as the 'Sangh Parivar' (family of the Rashtriya Swayamsevak Sangh, the RSS or National Volunteer Corps), including the Bharatiya Janata Party (BJP), the Bajrang Dal, and the Vishwa Hindu Parishad (VHP).

[2]   Such essentialism is not the monopoly of the Hindu Right, of course. Organisations such as Tablighi Jama'at work to expunge 'cultural' and 'religious' syncretism from Muslim practice in South Asia (Gardner 1999; Metcalf 1999). Some Muslim religious leaders claim that Muslims, as an endangered minority, must act as a unity, despite their internal differences and divisions: and that what happens to Muslim women should be the responsibility of Muslims alone.

[3]   Few Scheduled Caste people in Bijnor described themselves as Dalits ('Oppressed'). A few were neo-Buddhists. Scheduled Castes used to be called Untouchables or Harijans.

[4]   Such arguments ceased once Jats managed to achieve their own classification in UP as OBCs!

[5]   In this volume we mainly concentrate on the intersections of gender and communal identities and have put class and caste identities on one side.

6   Here we follow Bent Flyvbjerg in his powerful case for the necessity of case-study approaches for understanding and explanation in the social sciences (Flyvbjerg 2001; Flyvbjerg 2004; for the application of similar ideas to demography, see Greenhalgh 1995; Szreter et al. 2004).

'WE FIVE, OUR TWENTY-FIVE'
MYTHS OF POPULATION OUT OF CONTROL
IN CONTEMPORARY INDIA

Charan Singh:[1] I have three sons – the third came in the foolishness of looking for a girl. I will try to educate them all to MA level in the hope that they will get service. It doesn't matter if they all go away to work, I can always employ someone to do the farm work. Unless they get a good job, what benefit will there be from the education? Fortunately, my wife can supervise the children's study; I myself don't have the time.

Roger: Why did you want a girl?

Charan Singh: First to help her mother in the house, before she is married; secondly because if there is any work to be done (like getting a glass of water or some food) a girl will never refuse but a son will; also a daughter is needed for me to get the merit of giving a daughter in marriage.

Roger: Why not have only one son, then he would get all the land?

Charan Singh: Like I said, I need more than one in case that one son is bad.

Roger: Then why not have many more sons?

> **Charan Singh:** Yes, that would be good for making the country
> strong; and would be important, for example in fighting, like
> against the Muslims, because their population is growing faster.
> But children are too expensive: the everyday costs are so high
> I couldn't afford any more.

Fertility in India has been declining since the early 1970s
and numerous recent studies indicate that many people
say that they can afford only a few children. In the same
period, family planning has been ineluctably flavoured
by the communa-lisation of politics at both national and
grassroots levels, with the widespread belief that Indian
Muslims oppose family planning and do not adhere to the
often-expressed ideal of 'two boys and a girl'. Thus, this
interchange with a Hindu middle-to-rich peasant farmer
from the locally dominant Jat caste in Bijnor district encapsulates important themes in current understandings of
India's fertility transition – a transition that seems to be
slower in UP than in most of the rest of India.

The first section of this chapter outlines 'myths of
population out of control', especially those about the
scale and causes of fertility differentials between Hindus
and Muslims that are associated with the so-called Hindu
Right. These ideas have a commonsense quality, a pervasive but misplaced credibility, even for people with no
active involvement in Hindu Right politics. The second
section begins to challenge these views by examining
how demographers have addressed Hindu-Muslim fertility
through themes like regional differences, and variations
in socio-economic position and occupation, rather than
religion as such. We are broadly sympathetic to their approach, yet demographers' elaborate statistical analyses on

large-scale data sets are not readily sensitive to local-level variations. To conclude, we turn to our research in rural Bijnor to shed light both on Hindu Right political rhetoric and on the limitations of macro-level demographic analyses.

Communal Politics and the Numbers Game

The Hindu Right comprises several organisations, including the Bharatiya Janata Party (BJP), Rashtriya Swayamsevak Sangh (RSS or National Volunteer Corps), Vishwa Hindu Parishad (VHP) and their associated women's and youth organisations. These organisations epitomise an explicitly Hindu nationalist stance (as distinct from Nehru's 'secular' nationalism). For instance, during the 1980s, they spearheaded a campaign to remove the Babari Masjid (a 16th century mosque in Ayodhya), claiming that it was built over the birthplace of the Hindu god Ram. Their supporters demolished the mosque in 1992 and anti-Muslim riots flared around India.[2] A coalition led by the BJP (the Hindu Right's main political party) was in power in UP from 1997-2002, and its leader was the Indian Prime Minister from 1998-2004.

During the 1980s and 1990s, the Hindu Right echoed allegations repeatedly made in Hindu nationalist discourse since the early 20th century that Muslims constitute a threat to the 'Hindu community' (Datta 1993). A heightened preoccu-pation with 'community' numbers and population growth rates has been linked to colonial census operations and other aspects of British rule, especially from the latter part of the 19th century onwards (Appadurai 1993; Cohn 1987; Jones 1981; Pandey 1990). During the 20th century, Hindu nationalist claims have focused inter alia on Muslim expansionism through invasions, forced conversions, and the abduction of Hindu women, and have characterised Muslim men as militant, sexually predatory, and a danger to India's integrity (Bacchetta 1994; Bacchetta 1996; Basu 1993; Gupta 1998; Gupta 2002: 222-320; Jaffrelot 1996b; Pandey 1991). This discourse also portrays Indian Muslims as complicit with Pakistan, with their efforts to boost Muslim numbers supposedly entailing the conversion of poor Hindus (financed with Gulf state money), and schemes to infiltrate Muslims from Pakistan and Bangladesh into India (Basu 1996: 132-135; Basu et al. 1993: 74-75; Gupta & Sharma 1996; Jaffrelot 1996b: 338ff.; Wright 1983).[3]

To argue on the Hindu Right's chosen ground of contrasting the demographic profiles of religious communities risks conceding that "the philosophical postulates of a particular religion.... constitute the exclusive, unchanging organisational principles for an entire people across all kinds of spaces, times and historical change" (Basu et al. 1993: 74). Differences in life-chances within the categories 'Hindu' and 'Muslim', however, are likely to be as significant as variations between the two categories. Essentialising Hindu and Muslim demographic behaviour, though, is part of the Hindu Right's strategy to gain and retain political power, by creating an 'Other' and reinforcing their own claim to represent all who regard themselves as Hindu. Given the Hindu Right's central role in contemporary Indian politics, we would be evading our academic responsibilities if we refused to confront their myths of population out of control – even if, in doing so, we risk being mired in the numbers game (compare Basu 1996: 154).

Islam and Family Planning

An enduring feature of the Hindu Right's anti-Muslim rhetoric is that Indian Muslims have a grand plan to render Hindus a minority in their 'own country', a claim that relies heavily on asserting that Muslim fertility is significantly higher than that of Hindus. Since the early 1970s, Hindu Right propaganda has also vigorously insisted that Indian Muslims are antinational because of their supposed refusal to adopt 'modern' contraception (for example, Hendre 1971; Prakash 1979; see Basu 1997; Basu 1996; Wright 1983 for appraisals). Indeed, some Hindu religious leaders, with support from communal political parties (Jana Sangh [now BJP] and Shiv Sena), have advocated population growth for Hindus to avert the purported threat of being outnumbered (Mandelbaum 1974: 105).[4]

The view that Islamic doctrine opposes family planning and that Muslims docilely respond to their religious leaders' propaganda draws on (and feeds into) a much wider pattern of portraying Muslims as dominated by Islam. Yet comparable assumptions are rarely made about adherents of other religions. Extrapolations are drawn from a few Islamic theologians, with little thought to their social locations, to disputes among different schools of Islamic thought, to changes through time, or to the complex relationships between theology and everyday social practices.[5]

Through the centuries, Islamic texts have lent themselves to diverse theological stances on family planning. Omran, for instance, focuses on the lack of clarity in Islamic texts over the acceptability of different forms of contraception, notes that some sources condone coitus interruptus and suggests (by extension) that all forms of non-terminal family planning are acceptable (Omran 1992). Some theologians have regarded abortion as acceptable before 'ensoulment', which occurs after the third month of pregnancy. Some authorities consider wanting to avoid poverty or to raise family living standards unacceptable motives for sterilisation, whereas wishing to avoid endangering the mother's health or transmitting a serious disease can be morally justified. Theological objections raised about sterilisation – that the permanent prevention of conception signifies a lack of faith in God's capacity to provide – are most powerfully expressed, and it seems not to be actively endorsed by any school of Islamic jurisprudence (Khan 1979: 184-191).[6]

In South Asia, Maulana Maudoodi argued in Radiance (the Jama'at-i Islami journal) that birth control produces sexual anarchy (Wright 1983). In Pakistan, though, Maudoodi's position was not influential, and other Islamic leaders there have not denounced sterilisation in particular, despite their generalised opposition to the government's family planning programmes. In Bangladesh, the steep decline in the Total Fertility Rate and the rise in contraceptive prevalence rates since the early 1970s undermine the view that doctrinal opposition prevents South Asian Muslims from adopting family planning (Caldwell et al. 1999; Levin et al. 1999). In several other Muslim-majority countries, large numbers of men and women have undergone sterilisation, including Iran, where it was banned after the Revolution of 1979 but made available again after 1989 (Obermeyer 1994).

In India, some Muslim religious leaders have suggested that the political Emergency (1975-1977) was an era when family planning staff and other government workers disproportionately targeted Muslims for sterilisation. Some Muslim clerics, indeed, have claimed that family planning (especially sterilisation) is contrary to Islam, but their failure to endorse the Indian government's family planning programme reflects the politics of minority status. Indian Muslims' fertility behaviour cannot be attributed to a supposedly universal and timeless Islamic condemnation of contraception in general, or of sterilisation in particular (Basu 1996: 139-141). In any case, if Muslim religious leaders in India condemn contraception, we must ask how far their audiences take this into consideration in their own fertility behaviour (compare Cassen 1978: 56). This question is further complicated by the Indian family planning programme's obsession with sterilisation (see below).

The 'Backward' Muslim Woman and Polygamy

From the mid 19th century, Christian missionaries and local reformers alike condemned the seclusion of women (purdah) for causing health problems, endangering women in childbirth, preventing girls from attending school, and ensuring that their 'backwardness' would continue to undermine their role as mothers (Lal 1999; Minault 1998; Savage 1997). The most strictly secluded were women from the elite classes, whether Muslim or Hindu. In practice, then, purdah was not an Islamic institution, though it was often (erroneously) said to have been introduced into India by Muslim invaders.

A key strand in the Hindu Right's recent rhetorical demonisation of Indian Muslims is that purportedly Islamic institutions, such as purdah, victimise Muslim women and perpetuate their 'backwardness'. This echoes (though with a communalist spin) contemporary demographers' preoccu-pations with the links between women's 'autonomy', girls' schooling, and fertility (see below). Hindu Right claims about Muslim women's 'backwardness', however, have generally been more indirectly linked to fertility through discourses on polygamy. Muslim men are stereotyped as more sexually active than Hindu men and as wanting more sexual partners and more children from them. Muslim women are cast as victims of Muslim men's (supposedly) excessive sexual appetites.[7]

Despite the Hindu Right's complaints about Muslim polygamous marriages (and the censorious comments of many high caste Hindus in Bijnor about Muslims and polygamy), the proportion of Muslim men with more than one wife is very small. Indeed, in India in the 1970s, the rate of polygamy among Muslims was somewhat less than among Hindus, for all that it is supposedly illegal for Hindus (Krishnakumar 1991; National Committee on the Status of Women 1975: 21-23, 40-42). In rural Bijnor, polygamy is still very uncommon and still occurs about equally among Muslims and Hindus.[8] Ethnographic accounts of Indian Muslims generally make only passing reference to polygamy. In practice, of course, there could be many polygamous marriages among Muslims only if Muslim men were marrying much younger women, or if (as the Hindu Right sometimes claims) women from other 'communities' were converting and marrying Muslim men.

There is, however, no credible evidence of conversions on a scale sufficient to create significant demographic shifts. In addition, the suggested link between polygamy and raised levels of fertility is problematic: what little evidence there is suggests that women in polygamous marriages usually have fewer not more children than comparable women in monogamous unions (Basu 1997: 10-11; Basu 1996: 138-139).[9] In any case, polygamy has long been extremely contentious among Muslims. Conservatives generally say that Islam permits but does not actively encourage polygamy. Modernists argue that the Qur'anic verse that apparently permits polygamy sets such stringent conditions (that a man treat his wives equally) that it is effectively a prohibition, unless there are exceptional circumstances.[10]

Hindu Right rhetoric, then, rests on two crucial but false assumptions: that polygamy is common among Muslims but unknown among Hindus and that it is associated with high levels of fertility. Nevertheless, in 1968, the Organiser (the RSS journal) asserted that Muslims were using polygamy to activate the population bomb as a war tactic against Hindus (cited in Bacchetta 1994: 198). During the Babari Masjid campaign of 1986-92, Sadhvi Saraswati claimed that polygamy "turns Muslim women into sexual objects and breeders", that for every five Hindu children born, Muslims have fifty, and that Hindus would become a minority in India within twenty-five years (Basu 1999: 173; see also Basu 1996: 137). Sadhvi Ritambhara asserted:

> The Muslims got their Pakistan. Even in a mutilated India, they have special rights. They have no use for family planning. They have their own religious schools. What do we have? An India with its arms cut off. ... The state tells us Hindus to have

> only two or three children. After a while they will say 'do not
> have even one'. But what about those who have six wives,
> 30-35 children, and breed like mosquitoes and flies? (Quoted
> in Kakar 1995: 207-08).

The Indian government's family planning slogan advocating a small family norm for everyone – 'ham do, hamåre do' ('we two, our two') with its logo of a couple with their two children – has had a public presence across India, from the walls of government buildings to postage stamps and railway tickets. The Hindu Right's distorted appropriation of this slogan neatly encapsulates their fallacies about Muslims and polygamy. A VHP pamphlet published in 1990 contained the riposte: while Hindus (supposedly) obey the government's slogan, Muslim men allegedly have four wives and say, 'ham pånch, hamåre pachðs' ('we five, our twenty-five') (see Gupta 2002: 4; Sarkar 1993: 165).

This slogan and the assumptions that Islam is set against contraception and that Muslim men marry polygamously have attained a taken-for-granted quality. Paola Bacchetta and Pradip Datta (personal communications) both suggest that such claims do not figure as centrally in official publications of Hindu Right organisations (such as the RSS) as in verbal discourse, whether interviews or speeches made at rallies and other gatherings. Moreover, "a trope of extinction" (Datta 1999: 23) has become part of the "common truth, a product of social 'good sense'" (Datta 1993: 1305) beyond Hindu Right activists (see also Wright 1983). Certainly, we often heard views such as these in Bijnor in 1990-1991 and in our subsequent research in 2000-2002, whether from urban middle class people, or from villagers such as Charan Singh. Few were paid-up or active members of any Hindu Right organisation (neither was Charan Singh).[11] Yet comments were often larded with the 'we five, our twenty-five' slogan, which was also blasted out by the tannoy system at the BJP offices in Bijnor town during the general election campaign in Spring 1991. Even some Muslims we talked to believed that Muslims would outstrip Hindus in the foreseeable future.[12] Crucially, the Hindu Right's narrative rests on the assertion that Indian Muslims' fertility behaviour is part of a plan to outnumber Hindus, a claim that rests on several demonstrably false premises and that seriously misrepresents complex social processes that influence fertility.

Demographers on Fertility Differentials

By contrast, demographers generally do not regard Islamic ideology as a key factor or, indeed, the categories 'Hindu' and 'Muslim' as sufficiently homogeneous for fertility differentials between them to be meaningfully analysed.[13] Demographers systematically disaggregate the categories 'Hindu' and 'Muslim' along socioeconomic lines – region, place of residence (urban or rural), occupation, education (especially of the mother), class – rather than positing essential differences on the basis of religion per se. Thus they tend to undermine the very notion of 'Muslim fertility'. Further, they examine the impact of polygamy, along with, for instance, age of marriage, length of breast-feeding, length of postpartum sexual abstinence, or other periods of sexual abstinence. But they treat these as proximate variables affecting fertility without making any assumptions about people's intentions. In recent years, demographers have also focused on gender politics, but in a decidedly different fashion from the Hindu Right. The findings of academic demographers, then, provide compelling critiques of the Hindu Right's simplistic claims about Hindu-Muslim differences in fertility behaviour.

Region, Class, and Fertility

At the macro-level, Indian demographic statistics indicate that Muslim fertility rates are somewhat higher than those among Hindus, and that Muslims make up a (slowly) growing share of the Indian population (up from 10.7 per cent in 1961 to 13.4 per cent in 2001).[14] Apart from some small-scale surveys and local case studies, demographers have mainly relied on special national surveys (International Institute for Population Studies 1995; Registrar General India 1976; Registrar General India 1982) and the 1981, 1991 and 2001 national censuses for their analyses of inter-religious fertility differentials in India.[15] Selecting only one indicator (total fertility rate, TFR), the Infant and Child Mortality Survey produced all-India estimates for 1978 for rural Muslim TFRs about 12 per cent above those of Hindus (5.01 compared to 4.48) and somewhat more than 12 per cent for urban residents (3.98 compared to 2.97) (Registrar General India 1982: 6).[16]

Disaggregated figures, however, provide a more complex picture. The regional distribution of Muslims is uneven: in 1981, 36 per cent of them lived in Bihar and Uttar Pradesh, which accounted for only 27 per cent of India's total population. These northern states have higher fertility and mortality rates than the rest of the country: the 1978 estimated rural TFR for Muslims was 6.39 and for Hindus was 5.82 in UP, whereas in Tamil Nadu the TFRs were 3.64 and 3.43 respectively; the urban rates were 3.88 and 3.21 in UP and 3.24 and 2.67 in Tamil Nadu. That is, Hindu fertility rates in north India are often higher than Muslim rates in central, eastern, and south India.[17] The national surveys also show sizable statistical effects for the literacy level of the mother, age at marriage, and total household expenditure, all of which are greater than the inter-religious differentials.

Within north India, Muslims are more urbanised than Hindus (in UP 36 per cent of Muslims lived in towns in 2001, compared to 17 per cent of Hindus), but urban Muslims disproportionately occupy poorer housing areas with lower levels of public health infrastructure and have lower-paid jobs than their Hindu neighbours. More than half of urban Muslims are reported to have incomes below the poverty line, compared to 35 per cent of urban Hindus. In 1978, 79 per cent of rural Muslim households owned less than one hectare, compared to 68 per cent of rural Hindu households (Krishnakumar 1991; Shariff 1995; Sridhar 1991). In brief, Muslims are poorer and less educated than Hindus, as well as being distributed differently across the country.

Published analyses of the 1992-1993 data provided all-India comparisons of TFR (4.41 for Muslims and 3.30 for Hindus) though urban and rural rates by state were not systematically produced (Moulasha & Rao 1999).[18] Regional differences in fertility levels were still clear-cut (Bhat & Zavier 1999). Multivariate analysis of the independent role of religion was done only for contraceptive use – and then only controlling for education and region separately, and not for socioeconomic status (Ramesh &

Retherford 1996).[19] The independent effect of religion, holding constant a wide range of other variables, was not systematically analysed and discussed until 2005.[20]

Large-scale survey data, then, indicated that there were inter-religious fertility differentials in the 1970s, 1980s and 1990s, but not whether they would remain or how large they would be after controlling for other important variables. An alternative approach was to use the 1981 and 1991 census data to calculate correlations between district-level characteristics and fertility, mortality, and female disadvantage (for example, Drèze & Murthi 1999; Kishor 1993; Bhat 1996; Bhat & Zavier 1999; Murthi et al. 1996). Sometimes religion was not mentioned at all (for example, Murthi et al. 1996) or only in passing (Kishor 1993). Others showed that the Muslim proportion of a district's population correlated positively with fertility indicators, even after controlling for other indicators (Drèze & Murthi 1999; Bhat 1996).[21] In these and other studies, urban-rural residence, women's labour force participation, and mother's schooling have been the key indicators analysed. Though the details are complex, demographers' analyses of large-scale data sets controlling for a range of social and economic variables significantly (but not wholly) reduce the Hindu-Muslim fertility differentials much trumpeted by the Hindu Right.

Women's 'Autonomy' and Fertility

Since the early 1980s, 'women's autonomy', or their capacity to make important decisions about their own lives, has been a preoccupation in demography. Most recent discussions focus on domestic politics – marriage arrangement, women's control over domestic resources, controls over women's mobility – as in Dyson and Moore's classic contribution (Dyson & Moore 1983). During the 1980s, labour force participation was considered crucial in enhancing women's domestic position and was central to discussions of regional differences in women's autonomy and discrimination against girls (Bardhan 1974; Miller 1981). But the unreliability of indicators of labour force participation derived from the Census proved a major limitation. It has rarely been treated seriously as an explanatory variable (e.g. by Kishor 1993), although the National Family Health Survey suggested that "only 15 per cent of the Muslim women participated in work whereas for Hindu women the figure was 34 per cent" (Moulasha & Rao 1999: 3048).

One of the most robust statistical relationships, however, is between girls' schooling and fertility decline. During the 1990s, extending girls' access to schooling became central in policy initiatives aimed at enhancing young women's autonomy, particularly with respect to fertility decision making. For India as a whole, survey and census data alike show that Muslims have less schooling than Hindus, reflecting and contributing to Muslims' generally weaker economic positions. Age for age, in rural and urban areas alike, a smaller proportion of Muslim than Hindu children is currently attending schools of any kind (Krishnakumar 1991; Shariff 1995). Up to age nine, approximately equal percentages of Hindu and Muslim boys (urban and rural) attend school; for girls, the situation is comparable, although the percentages of girls at school are lower. For older rural children, however, the gap between Muslim and Hindu enrolment levels widens markedly, especially for girls. In part, this reflects the relative concentration of Muslims in north India, where overall school enrolment rates are lower than elsewhere. Within north India, however, Muslim schooling rates are below those of Hindus in the same class position, especially for schooling beyond primary level.

Some demographic literature on the Middle East claims that features of gender politics that supposedly reduce Muslim women's autonomy (particularly seclusion) are key to understanding continuing high levels of fertility in the region.[22] Generally, though, analyses of women's autonomy have not regarded religious allegiance as a key issue. Krishnakumar (1991) and Alaka Basu (1996) are unusual in the emphasis they place on lower levels of literacy among Muslim women in India as a cause of higher fertility. Dyson and Moore (1983: 53), by contrast, concluded that religious identification had relatively little influence on female autonomy, their main explanatory variable for demographic differences between north and south India.

Population increase, of course, is also a matter of mortality and migration. There is little information on mortality rates by religion in India. Infant death rates are higher in the north than in the south, yet, for the country as a whole, Muslim infant mortality rates were about 109 per 1,000 live births in 1978, compared with about 121 per 1,000 live births for Hindus, a difference of 10 to 12 per cent (Registrar General India 1981). Moulasha and Rama Rao (1999: 3049) suggest that the child survival rate of children born to Muslim mothers was 20 per cent above that of children born to Hindu mothers in 1992. Unfortunately, there are few good multivariate analyses that combine factors like region, rural-urban residence, schooling of parents, and economic position to determine the net relationships between religion and mortality. Considering the large contribution of infant and child mortality to total mortality, though, Muslim total mortality might also be around 10 per cent below that of Hindus. If so, this could be almost as significant (in terms of differentials in population totals) as fertility differences but, unlike fertility, mortality has not been politicised by the Hindu Right. For most of India, migration rates are too small to be demographically significant (Moulasha & Rao 1999: 3047), but migration has become politically contentious, with widespread anxiety about the infiltration of people from Bangladesh. In western UP, though, local migration patterns have not been an issue in communal politics.

In sum, demographic analyses have shown that Muslim and Hindu fertility levels alike are higher in rural areas, in north India, and among the poor and the poorly educated, than in urban areas, in south India, or among wealthier and educated couples, especially when the wife has more than eight years of schooling. After taking account of differences in the proportions who marry and in the age distributions of the two categories, fertility differences between religious communities can be largely (though not wholly) understood with reference to social and economic factors. Moreover, all these fertility rates are well below 'natural' fertility and fertility was declining for all groups at about the same rate in the 1980s and 1990s, albeit from different starting points. Even if Muslim fertility rates fall more slowly and Muslim mortality rates remain lower than Hindu rates, the Muslim proportion of India's population is unlikely to reach 15 per cent by 2021.[23] This contrasts markedly with Hindu Right rhetoric that reifies the categories 'Hindu' and 'Muslim', assumes a homogeneity and potency to Islamic ideology, and claims that Muslims will soon outnumber Hindus.

Muslim and Hindu in Rural Bijnor

We largely concur with demographers who argue that fertility differentials in India can largely be accounted for by analysing social and economic variables and that the role of religion per se is relatively limited. Yet something still needs to be explained, for fertility differentials remain – albeit much smaller than those implied by Hindu Right rhetoric – even after regional and socioeconomic variables have been taken into account.

In analysing our Bijnor data, however, we have become increasingly dissatisfied with conventional macro-demographic analysis. First, most demographers rely on special surveys or district-level data from the Census, but problems arise from working with units of analysis as large as a district (with perhaps several million people). When there is diversity below this level, excessive aggregation of data may mask variations between and within localities. Explanations of differences in fertility behaviour, then, cannot be meaningfully carried out at the level of nation or even region. Second, demographers conduct elaborate statistical techniques to try to separate out the main elements in a causal model of demographic change, as in the recent emphasis on the widespread, statistically significant correlation between girls' education and low fertility. But our fieldwork suggests that this correlation is not necessarily straightforwardly causal (see below).[24] In general, detailed micro-studies using local-level data and dealing with meaningful social groupings provide a better window into the fine-grain and locally specific processes that are likely to elude large-scale surveys. Differences exposed by large-scale statistical analyses, then, may suggest possible hypotheses, but not final answers.

Some social demographers, indeed, advocate amplifying data on measurable features of individuals (age at marriage, desired family size, and so on) derived from large-scale surveys with small-scale studies of the social relationships that link individuals' decisions (or non-decisions) to the collectivities to which they belong. Our experiences in rural Bijnor endorse Greenhalgh's view that we must "situate fertility, that is, to show how it makes sense given the socio-cultural and political economic context in which it is embedded" (Greenhalgh 1995: 17). By locating people's approaches to fertility in the context of rural Bijnor, our 'situated' account challenges both Hindu Right rhetoric and conventional demographers' accounts. We focus here on local perceptions of the family planning programme, examine aspects of gender politics and women's autonomy at the domestic level, and, finally, outline local understandings of social and economic exclusion.[25]

We conducted village surveys in 1990-1991 and interviewed people from many different caste and class backgrounds in rural Bijnor District. The material here, though, mainly concerns two roughly comparable caste groups, Sheikhs (Muslim) and Jats (Caste Hindu).[26] Muslims in Bijnor District, especially in urban areas, are particularly associated with artisanal and labouring activity. Rural Sheikhs, however, are the prime Muslim landowners in this part of the district, as are the Jats among

Caste Hindus. Among Sheikhs and Jats alike there are class differences (assessed largely in terms of land ownership). Even when class is held constant, though, Sheikh fertility is higher than Jat fertility. Hence, we must ask if there are features of the local situation that affect the Sheikhs as Muslims and contribute to their higher fertility.

Muslims and Family Planning in Rural Bijnor

The image of Muslims rejecting family planning because of Islamic doctrine and an ambition to outnumber Hindus is central to the Hindu Right perspective. Our data suggest that Sheikhs (indeed Muslims in general in rural Bijnor) did resist the government family planning programme, but mainly for reasons of quality of service and the contraceptive technologies being offered.

We frequently observed the supercilious and disdainful manner of medical and paramedical staff (who were usually Hindus from relatively high caste urban backgrounds), especially with respect to Muslim and poor Hindu villagers. Semi-public consultations compromised patient privacy and confidentiality, and women were often chided for their childcare practices or their repeated pregnancies. Local sensibilities about family planning were particularly acute, because government health staff have had 'targets' (the number of 'cases' they should motivate for family planning) throughout much of the period since the mid 1970s. Consultations would routinely be diverted onto family planning (for example, Najma's visit to an ophthalmologist, described in Jeffery & Jeffery 1996a: 53-68). Many Muslims to whom we talked thought they were singled out by family planning workers, as they believed they had been during the 1975-1977 Emergency, when health workers and other government staff were put under greatest pressure to meet family planning targets. Health staff and many Muslims had diametrically opposed understandings: the former often commented adversely on Muslim views about family planning, the latter described the family planning programme as a government initiative to eradicate Muslims. At the same time, health services in Muslim-dominated villages were of poorer quality than in Hindu-dominated villages. Many Muslims complained that they were ignored in public health campaigns, such as immunisations, although some regarded such services as mere sweeteners to persuade people to accept family planning.

Mistrust of government health and family planning services was undoubtedly exacerbated by a bias toward sterilisation (overwhelmingly female sterilisation since the late 1970s), despite supposedly offering a 'cafeteria' service where people would select the family planning method that best suited their needs. Family planning workers not only had sterilisation targets but received incentive payments for every case they motivated (with lower payments for IUCD or intrauterine contraceptive devices); family planning acceptors also received small sums after sterilisation or IUCD insertion. Pressure on staff was such that they sometimes exaggerated their achievements in the health centre records (see Jeffery et al. 1989; Narayana & Kantner 1992 provide the national picture). Until the late 1980s, people in rural Bijnor generally thought that family planning and sterilisation were synonymous and that family planning staff could or would offer only sterilisation. Certainly, some women had IUCDs inserted and the contraceptive pill was available from pharmacies in Bijnor town, but a few women who wished their IUCD to be replaced or who wanted antenatal tetanus injections reported being pressured to become a sterilisation 'case'. Many people, especially poor Hindus and Muslims, feared being coerced into adopting terminal methods such as sterilisation. Although most women would have preferred spacing methods, mainly because of their fear of child mortality, it was widely considered futile to try to obtain them from family planning staff.

This led to popular resistance, as witness the requests we received during our research for alternative contra-ceptive methods, from Muslim and Hindu women alike. Certainly, rather than wanting numerous children, many of the Muslim women we talked to wished to limit their fertility, often pointing to the health costs to themselves and their children of repeated childbearing. Crucially, too, our data indicate significantly higher rates of infant and child mortality among rural Muslims in Bijnor than among comparable Hindus, in contrast to all-India statistics.

For Muslims in rural Bijnor, part of the story, but only a part, was certainly their belief that Islam prohibits ster-ilisation and that they should not use the family planning method most readily available through the government health services (Jeffery & Jeffery 1996b; Jeffery & Jeffery 1997). But our field notes indicate that their reactions to the family planning programme cannot be largely (leave aside wholly) attributed to their understandings of Is-lamic doctrine. The Muslims we talked to in rural Bijnor approached fertility limitation in a similar fashion to that of most of the other groups in the locality, with no gener-alised resistance to spacing methods of fertility limitation, but with an aversion to terminal methods and a mistrust of the government's family planning programme. In other words, our research indicates that many women's needs for acceptable contraception were far from being met.

The Jats presented a striking contrast to this picture. Far more of them were actively limiting their families than were Muslims as a whole (including Sheikhs) and Hindus from the smaller, poorer, and lower castes. Of the Jat women we interviewed in 1991, 59 per cent of those aged 35 to 45 and 42 per cent of those aged 25 to 35 were using some form of modern contraception. They accessed health care and contraceptive services, including pills, IUCDs, and female sterilisation via government family planning services as well as local private doctors. Does this mean, then, that instead of trying to account for the fertility differentials between Sheikhs and Jats in rural Bijnor in terms of Islamic doctrine, we should focus on women's capacity to implement their family planning preferences?

Women's Autonomy, Education, and Fertility in Rural Bijnor

Deconstructing the household can show that household members (such as husbands and wives) may have con-flicting as well as common interests (see Chapter 2 of this volume for more discussion of this point).[27] Gender politics at the household level, then, are likely to be crucial in many matters, including family planning decisions: as Greenhalgh (1995: 14) argues, reproduction is a "deeply gendered process". In recent demographic discussions of women's autonomy and fertility decline, girls' education has been a central concern.

In line with the national picture outlined above, girls from different castes and communities in rural Bijnor tend to have had different schooling experiences. Most Jat women had attended school. Sizable numbers, disproportionately from the wealthiest households, had obtained post-school qualifications such as BA or MA. By contrast, not even Sheikh women from rich peasant households were likely to have been educated outside the home. Those few who did attend school usually went to a madrasah (mosque school) rather than a secular school. Might the fertility differentials between rural Sheikhs and Jats that remained after controlling for class be attributed to different schooling experiences and different levels of autonomy among adult women?

Unfortunately, demographers have tended to treat both 'education' (usually glossed as 'years of schooling') and 'autonomy' as black boxes that are simple variables consistently and causally linked to one another and to fertility. Thus Drèze and Murthi (1999: 3), for example, find that "women's education emerges as the most important factor explaining fertility differences across the country and over time." A local-level perspective, however, indicates that 'autonomy' and 'education' and their inter-relationships are far more complex than this.

In rural Bijnor, it is doubtful that schooling experiences in themselves provided women with the capacity to act autonomously. School curricula, styles of classroom interaction, and the body language inculcated in girls at school seemed more likely to sustain conventional gender hierarchies than to enhance girls' autonomy, in the sense of capacity to think and act independently. At a madrasah, girls had to cover their heads and behave demurely while learning to recite the Qu'rån Sharðf; the wider curriculum did not always include Hindi and other subjects that might give access to knowledge beyond Islåmiyåt (Islamic ideas and history); and madrasah schooling was usually terminated once girls reached puberty. Secular schools also provided little scope for ensuring that pupils graduated with enhanced autonomy. In addition, many rural women who studied to BA and MA levels had done so as 'private' rather than 'regular' students, that is by corres-pondence courses at home – hardly an effective way of honing the skills and confidence to deal with the world beyond the home that are so often considered an important consequence of school attendance. Moreover, it was abundantly clear that parents did not send daughters to school in order to create autonomous women. Obtaining qualifications for paid employment was almost never considered (although some people said qualifications might enable a woman to stand on her 'own legs' after a calamity such as widowhood or divorce). Rather, parents saw their daughters' schooling as a newly important (and quite costly) asset in the marriage market.

Measuring 'education' in terms of 'years of schooling', then, simply cannot grasp the local meanings attached to girls' schooling or the contrasts between different types of schools or different locations in which girls study. In any case, even if schooling could enable girls to think more independently, educated Jat women had no more control over the choice of their marriage partner or the timing of their marriage than women with little or no schooling. In rural Bijnor, young married women of all castes and communities, for whom decisions about fertility were particularly salient, operated within broadly comparable forms of domestic gender politics.

It is generally assumed that purdah disempowers women, for it restricts their mobility outside the home and may imply their lack of involvement in paid employment that could provide independent income. For the Hindu Right, purdah is a marker of Muslim women's 'backwardness', but many ethnographic studies report on seclusion and veiling practices among Hindus, albeit often pointing to subtle differences between Hindu and Muslim purdah (see Jacobson & Wadley 1995; Mandelbaum 1986; Mandelbaum 1988; Papanek 1982). Certainly, our data do not support an argument that Sheikh women (or indeed Muslim women as a whole) were more restricted by seclusion practices than Jat women (or Hindu women in general). Rather, seclusion practices reflected local ideas about family honour that were common to Hindus and Muslims.

Adult women's mobility beyond the domestic domain reflected differing work demands (relating primarily to the household's class position) and household composition and a woman's position in it (for example, as sole adult woman, or as mother-in-law or daughter-in-law), not religious allegiance. In the wealthiest rural households, women worked inside the house but rarely outside. In poorer households, women often had to work outside, whether as family labour or as employees of wealthier households in the locality, but such mobility was limited to the task at hand and did not imply enhanced autonomy or freedoms. One feature of gender politics remained constant, however: land, the major economic resource, was owned (albeit very inequitably) by men and not by women. Few women had any independent income; employed women worked out of necessity but usually earned very little as they had no marketable skills aside from domestic or farming work. Sheikh and Jat women as a whole, then, were not systematically differentiated in terms of mobility beyond the home, access to land and independent income: such contrasts as were present reflected class rather than community differences.

Our data highlight an additional problem with assuming that 'education' straightforwardly enhances young married women's autonomy in their marital homes. The most educated Jat women were married into the richest households and were expected to be home-based. They were also more likely to be married to an only son and thus required to share a household with their mother-in-law. Yet women of all castes and communities thought sharing a household with the mother-in-law was more constricting than running their own household. Thus, girls' education neither correlates convincingly with differences in women's 'autonomy' nor provides us with much insight into the fertility differentials between Jats and Sheikhs in rural Bijnor.

Further, low school attendance by Sheikh and other Muslim girls cannot readily be explained by purdah restrictions (or Muslim 'backwardness'). For many Muslim families, poverty was an important restraint on sending children to school. For more wealthy Muslims, though, low school attendance by girls reflected (among other things) the lower likelihood for state schools to be located in Muslim villages or Muslim areas of mixed villages. Additionally, Muslim parents believed that Muslim girls were sexually and communally harassed at school and that the madrasah provided a more appropriate curriculum in a more protected envi-ronment.

None of these observations means that gender politics within the household are unimportant in decisions about girls' education (or fertility) in rural Bijnor. They do require, though, that we locate individual behaviour and household dynamics within social and economic processes and relations of difference and inequality beyond the household (McNicoll 1994).

Perceptions of Exclusion in Rural Bijnor

For Greenhalgh (1995:21), fertility transitions are the "products of changes in class-specific opportunity structures in response to transformations of global and regional political economies". Here, then, we want to account for the fertility differentials between Sheikhs and Jats in rural Bijnor in terms of their contrasting locations in local social and economic structures. We focus on the social and political implications of labelling oneself and being labelled by others as 'Muslim' in rural Bijnor, not on Muslims as adherents of stereotyped Islamic spiritual beliefs and doctrinal commands.

Dyson considers that high fertility among poor rural populations does not need much explanation, largely because few people are making active decisions about family sizes. Fertility levels may be lower than 'natural' fertility, but they may reflect unintentional factors such as age at marriage, length of breast-feeding, or sexual abstinence, rather than purposeful contraceptive use. By contrast, low or declining fertility in some sectors of the population does need explanation (Dyson 1991).

Were some Hindus in rural Bijnor, notably the Jats, experiencing social processes that led them to favour small families, whereas Muslims were not? As elsewhere in India, Muslims in rural Bijnor tended to be poorer and less educated. But school attendance by Muslim boys was lower than for Hindu boys even when class was held constant. Sheikh and Jat parents alike saw boys' schooling primarily as a resource in the job market and secondarily as an element in marriage arrangements. Charan Singh's comment quoted above is typical: "Unless they get a good job, what benefit will there be from the education?" Jats were generally optimistic that schooling enhances (though does not guarantee) the chances of obtaining white collar employment. Crucially, however, Sheikhs in Bijnor did not believe that their sons would get good jobs, no matter how much schooling they received. Sheikhs generally did not spend as much money on their children's schooling or put as much pressure on their children to attend school as did the Jats. Although Sheikh parents' views about schooling might adversely affect their sons' job prospects, several pointers suggest that the reverse is more plausible – that Sheikhs' experiences of exclusion from the job market led them to put a lower value on schooling than do comparable Hindus.

First, Muslims are not covered by job quotas in government services, in contrast to the Scheduled Castes and Tribes and the Other Backward Castes. Nowadays, the practical significance of such exclusion is questionable, since there are very few 'reserved' posts available. Nevertheless, many Muslims in Bijnor felt that their exclusion reflected other aspects of the Indian government's attitude toward Muslims. Second, our Muslim and Hindu informants generally claimed that job applicants in the public and private sectors alike needed either influence (sifårish) through caste, kinship, or religious community networks or cash for a bribe (rishwat) or both to have much chance of being appointed. Firm evidence for these claims is hard to find. Yet the belief in such processes was crucial in parents' calculations about the value of investing in their sons' schooling. The absence (perceived or real) of Muslims in key positions damaged Muslims' access to future appointments, directly (because Muslim applicants have few people over whom they can exert 'influence') and indirectly (by disheartening students and their parents at crucial stages of their progress through schooling). This also applied, of course, to poor Hindus who lacked the necessary networks and cash.

In addition, schooling is not standardised. Wealthier families, rural as well as urban, would pay for private schooling and for 'tuition' after school hours for their sons, and would expect women of the family to supervise children's homework. Poor rural families, however, could access only poor quality schooling and their low levels of social and cultural capital also restricted what their sons could gain from schooling. Muslims were differentially disadvantaged by poverty, yet, prior to 2000 and unlike children from the Scheduled Castes and Tribes, they were not entitled to scholarships and fee waivers. Madrasah schooling may have been more financially accessible, but it fed only into theological training and employment as an imåm for a few able boys. Further, many Muslims believed that the ambience of mainstream schools was hostile to Islam and that Muslim children were subjected to harassment from other pupils and teachers alike. They faced an uphill struggle to keep their sons in school and to help them to succeed, and this struggle often hardly felt worthwhile, because the rewards, in terms of secure employment, seemed so elusive.

Girls' schooling certainly enters people's calculations about fertility and schooling, but not in the direct way posited by the demographic orthodoxy. Girls' schooling was valued for its contribution to marriageability, not employability. All girls' schooling was conditioned by the need to educate them to a level just below that of the kind of boy to whom their parents hoped to arrange their marriages. For many Jat girls, this could entail lengthy schooling and even college education. By contrast, Muslim girls' problems of harassment and of access to schools were compounded by the low levels of school attendance by Muslim boys, even among the relatively wealthy.

The crucial factor differentiating the fertility regimes of the Jats and the Sheikhs, however, was the Jats' relative success in the off-farm employment market. Most Jat men were limiting their families in pursuit of household goals: to educate their sons and place them in good employment, and to educate their daughters and arrange their marriages to educated young men with off-farm employment who would command increasingly larger dowries. Jat parents, then, obeyed the dictates of their pockets rather than the government's family planning slogan. As Charan Singh put it, "But children are too expensive: the everyday costs are so high I couldn't afford any more." By contrast, the Sheikhs lacked access to influential people, and processes of exclusion from sought-after employment effectively reduced the costs of child-rearing (school fees, bribes, dowry, for instance). Sheikh men were not unthinking followers of maulvǒs who (allegedly) told them to have large families. Rather, they remained locked into the agrarian economy. Investing in schooling made little sense and they had little incentive to limit their fertility – calculations that also applied to smaller and poorer Hindu and Muslim groups in rural Bijnor. In these respects, then, there was nothing essentially 'Muslim' about the Sheikhs' fertility regime.

Many Sheikh and other Muslim women articulated views on fertility akin to those of their husbands, emphasising Muslims' difficult social and economic position. In addition, because of low school attendance, Muslim girls were available for marriage at younger ages than comparable Hindu girls. Many Muslim women were dismayed by the damage to their own health and the heavy workloads caused by lengthy childbearing careers. Muslim women wanting contraception often had no option but subterfuge. By contrast, Jat couples generally made family planning decisions jointly. Jat women's wishes usually coincided with their husbands' plans, although a few Jat women could not have as many children as they themselves wanted because their in-laws wished to prevent land fragmentation and limit the costs of childrearing. In brief, Sheikh men did not especially oppress their womenfolk nor did Jat women have greater 'autonomy'. Rather, men's fertility rationales tended to prevail among Jats and Sheikhs alike.

Concluding Thoughts

The communalisation of politics in contemporary India has been buttressed by images of vulnerable Hindus (supposedly) doomed to be outnumbered. Assertions about Muslim fertility and about Muslim men's right to marry polygamously have been key to the Hindu Right's propaganda. Such communalist population myths are "short on facts, short on a proper understanding of the demographic situation – and short on honesty" (Krishnakumar 1991: 94) and dangerous propaganda in the victimisation of minority groups that contributes to creating the very differences that are used to justify demonising Muslims.

During our first fieldwork in Bijnor in 1982-1983, local Muslim commentaries on the family planning programme and on boys' employment prospects already exposed Muslims' sense of marginalisation and vulnerability. Political developments during the 1980s confirmed for them the government's ill intent toward Muslims and reinforced their distrust of the government machine. Muslims' insecurity was also exacerbated by sloganeering from the Hindu Right, by the communal disturbances in many parts of India during late 1990 (including in Bijnor: see Basu 1995c; Jeffery & Jeffery 1994b) and after the Babari Masjid was demolished in 1992, and by the BJP's subsequent electoral successes.

These physical and symbolic relations of dominance and subordination generated a sense of insecurity that structured the lives of Sheikhs in rural Bijnor qua Muslims. The expense of schooling children and accessing employment was linked to fertility behaviour just as much among Sheikhs as among Jat farmers, though with different outcomes. Far from higher fertility being an Islamic strategy for power or a plan to outbreed Hindus, it grew out of the Sheikhs' lack of power when compared with the locally dominant Jats.

Macro-level data, on which demographers typically rely, mask the fine-grain and complex processes that result in fertility differentials within a locality. The move away from the construction of grand narratives of fertility behaviour and toward 'situated' accounts, however, offers the promise of greater explanatory potential that could be used to good effect throughout South Asia (though with the details certainly differing from our account here). The move would be important for this reason alone. Given the politicisation of population issues in contemporary India, however, it has additional significance. 'Situated' accounts allow us to undermine the Hindu Right's views on Indian demography. Their views have achieved widespread acceptance and lie behind many acts of everyday routinised violence and discrimination against Muslims in India. It is thus imperative and politically urgent to challenge the Hindu Right's myths of Indian Muslims as a population out of control.

Notes

[1]   Charan Singh is a pseudonym. This is our translation from the Hindi.

[2]   On the Ayodhya affair and the communalisation of politics in contemporary India, see Basu & Kohli (1998); Basu et al. (1993); Chakravarti et al. (1992); Engineer (1991a); Gopal (1991); Hasan

(1997); Jaffrelot (1996a); Ludden (1996); van der Veer (1994); Vanaik (1997). The Ayodhya affair was linked to the Shah Bano case, which we consider in more detail in Chapter 2.

[3]   These allegations echo both the 'Islamophobia' currently widespread in the West and classically Orientalist arguments (Obermeyer 1992; Said 1978). Sikhs and Christians have sometimes been accused of undermining Hinduism through religious conversions and faster population growth rates, but Muslims were the target of most such claims in the 1990s (Krishnakumar 1991; van der Veer 1994; Wright 1983).

[4]   Similarly, reversing Hindu communalist messages, G. M. Shah argued that every Kashmiri Muslim should have a dozen children because they were dying out (Pai Panandikar & Umashankar 1994). Shah's demography was as incompetent as that of his Hindu Right opponents: the Muslim proportion in Jammu and Kashmir was 57 per cent in 1947 and 64 per cent in 1981.

[5]   For example, writing about the Middle East, Fargues draws links between Islamic fundamentalism, dreams of world conquest, and high fertility rates (Fargues 1993). Others highlight the tensions in Islamic doctrines between egalitarian and inegalitarian views and the "tremendous complexity and diversity that is found in the Muslim world" (Obermeyer 1994: 60; see also Ahmed 1982).

[6]   In 2004 a debate was launched within the All-India Muslim Private Law Board, between those (such as Kalbe Sadiq, the Shi'ite Vice-President) who argued that there was no objection within Islam to a two-child norm, and those (like Maulana Rabey Hasni Nadwi, the Chairman, and the Shahi Imam of Delhi) who see family planning as un-Islamic (Times of India, 16 September 2004).

[7]   Widow remarriage was also central to early 20th-century Hindu nationalist rhetoric. Muslim widows could remarry, whereas Hindu widows prevented from remarrying within their own community were allegedly lured into marriages with Muslim men. Either way, it was claimed, Muslim numbers would grow at the expense of Hindus. With declining levels of widowhood and rising levels of widow remarriage among Hindus, however, widow remarriage is no longer as contentious as it once was (Gupta 2002: 318, 324; see also Datta 1993; Davis 1951: 79-82; Mandelbaum 1974: 35).

[8]   On the other hand, Muslims and many Hindus in Bijnor comment adversely on de facto fraternal polyandry among the Jats, the dominant Hindu landholding group in the locality.

[9]   A first wife's failure to bear children (particularly a son) is a common reason for polygamy. Since male infertility may be the problem, second or later wives may also have difficulty in having children. Further, men marrying polygamously are generally older than those marrying for the first time and women in polygamous marriages are more likely to be widowed before menopause.

[10]   Ahmad discusses 19th-century modernist views (Ahmad 1967: 63, 73, 95), and Engineer provides a contemporary argument against polygamy (Engineer 1992: 22, 98ff., 154ff.).

[11]   Several young Jat men from his village, however, became involved in the Ayodhya campaign in late 1990, courting arrest in Bijnor town and attending political rallies.

[12]   Such claims make no sense nationally but local situations may seem less clear-cut. In Bijnor, for instance, 'caste Hindus' have gone from 46 per cent of the total District population in 1921 to about 35 per cent in 2001, and the Muslim share has risen from 36 per cent in 1921 to 42 per cent in 2001, despite some migration of Muslims to Pakistan in the late 1940s.

[13]   Three hypotheses linking fertility and religion have been distinguished (Goldscheider & Uhlenberg 1969). The first, 'particularised theology', attributes the effects of a religion to its doctrines about birth control and family size. The second, 'characteristics', explains religious differences in fertility through the social, economic, and demographic characteristics that the members of a particular religion happen to have. The third, 'minority group status', explains lower fertility among minority religious groups as a result of their insecurities. A fourth model describes 'interactions' that may change the relationships between fertility and religion through time (Chamie 1977). None of these is very satisfactory, either separately or together. We need a truly interactive model, one that acknowledges that "cultural, political, socio-economic, and historical factors interact with the relationship (between religion and fertility)" and that the "national and local context conditions the extent and perhaps nature of Islam's influence" (Knodel et al. 1999: 163).

[14] These figures include Assam and Jammu and Kashmir for both dates: see www.censusindia.net/religiondata/statement.pdf for more details.

[15] www.eastwestcenter.org/res-ph.asp provides data and reports from the 2nd National Family Health Survey, 1998-99.

[16] For more recent discussions of trends in fertility differentials by religion, see the Afterword to this volume and the special issue of Economic and Political Weekly, Vol. 40, no. 5 (2005).

[17] In these calculations, 'Hindu' includes 'Scheduled Castes' and 'Scheduled Tribes'.

[18] We have criticised their general approach in Jeffery & Jeffery (2000).

[19] In a small-scale study of rural Koil tehsil (Aligarh District, UP) the fertility differentials of caste Hindus, Scheduled Castes, and Muslims could be almost entirely understood in terms of the impacts of income, education, child mortality, and age at marriage (Khan 1991: 110-115).

[20] We discuss this debate in the Afterword to this volume.

[21] It is likely that Hindus in these districts have higher fertility than Hindus in other districts, and that Muslim fertility in these districts is at least as high, and probably higher, but it is not clear why this might be.

[22] Until the 1980s, Islamic countries in the Middle East were poor health achievers (relative to their wealth) and also, despite relatively high levels of female literacy, continued to have high levels of fertility. John Caldwell considered that "the central aspect of the relationship between Islam and mortality levels is undoubtedly the separate and distinctive position of women, operating partly through their access to education but also in many other ways" (Caldwell 1986: 175). He has now shifted position somewhat, because fertility levels in the region have dropped dramatically without apparently being accompanied by major social and economic changes, especially in relation to women's autonomy (Caldwell et al. 1999).

[23] Drèze and Murthi (1999) conclude that Muslims and Hindus differ neither in their preferences for sons nor in differentials in mortality rates by gender (see also Murthi et al. 1996). Sex ratios for Muslims in north India have historically been less 'masculine' than those for Hindus, probably because of differences in mortality rates overall

and the relationship of regional and socioeconomic factors to fertility (Agnihotri 2000).

[24] We have criticised this new orthodoxy elsewhere (Jeffery & Jeffery 1998; Jeffery & Basu 1996; see Drèze & Murthi 1999 for a response). Neither Drèze and Murthi nor Bhat (1996) elaborate on the correlation between high fertility and a high proportion of Muslims in a district, yet it is as strong as the links between girls' schooling and low fertility that are generally presumed to be causal.

[25] For further discussion of all these issues, see Chapter 3.

[26] This section draws on several of our publications on Bijnor (Jeffery 2000; Jeffery 2001; Jeffery & Jeffery 1994a; Jeffery & Jeffery 1996a; Jeffery & Jeffery 1996b; Jeffery et al. 1989; Jeffery & Jeffery 1993; Jeffery & Jeffery 1997). As we indicated above, polygamy is extremely rare in Bijnor, so we do not discuss it further here.

[27] See Agarwal (1997); Kandiyoti (1988); Kandiyoti (1998); Sen (1990) for elaborations of these issues, and also Kabeer (1999) on the problems of measuring women's empowerment and autonomy.

CHAPTER 2

A UNIFORM CUSTOMARY CODE?

MARITAL BREAKDOWN AND
WOMEN'S ECONOMIC ENTITLEMENTS

Among the many activities initiated during the British colonial era were the classification of the Indian population on the basis of religious allegiance and the codification of indigenous legal systems and customary means of dispute settlement.[1] These included procedures for dealing with family life – such as marriage and marital breakdown, child custody, and property transfers within the family. Recent commentaries note that written texts were privileged over oral traditions and that encoding the 'correct' legal framework entailed attempts to homogenise the diversity of 'customary practices'. Crucially, British civil servants consulting (male) religious experts assumed that family life was governed by religious texts. Thus, distinctive systems of 'personal law' were codified, despite considerable evidence of cultural parallels and religious syncretism. Further, official policy was that the authorities of the different religious communities should normally regulate their adherents' family life.[2] After 1947, the Hindu Code was revised, despite opposition (Agnes 1995; Kapur & Cossman 1996; Kishwar 1994; Parashar 1992) but Indian Muslims are still (notionally) governed by the Shariat Law of 1937.[3] Thus the multiplicity of 'personal laws' remains – enshrining religious or communal divisions through the differing rights, obligations and procedures for Indian citizens of different religions. The British rulers also developed systems of civil and criminal law applicable irrespective of religious allegiance, including the Criminal Procedure Code (CrPC). The Indian government's 1973 revisions of Section 125 of the CrPC enabled women who became homeless (for instance, after divorce or being ousted from a son's house) to press for maintenance from their ex-husband or their son.

How, though, should Muslim personal law and the CrPC come into play in relation to the rights of divorced Muslim women? It was this issue that rendered the case of Shah Bano, an elderly Muslim woman from Indore (in Madhya Pradesh) such a cause célèbre. After being divorced, Shah Bano appealed through the provisions of CrPC Section 125 for maintenance from her ex-husband.[4] He contested the case, claiming that it would be un-Islamic for a Muslim man to provide for his wife beyond the 'iddat period. The Supreme Court in Delhi adjudicated the case in 1985, but conservative Muslims argued that the (Hindu) Supreme Court judges had neither had the competence nor the jurisdiction to decide in Shah Bano's favour or to make adverse comments about women's position in Islam. Indeed, during this outcry, Shah Bano felt compelled to dissociate herself from the judgement because she came to believe that it was contrary to Islamic law (Engineer 1987: 211-2). Rajiv Gandhi's Congress government permitted an independent member of parliament to introduce the somewhat curiously titled Muslim Women (Protection of Rights on Divorce) Bill, which became law in 1986. Its provisions seemed to protect Muslim men from maintenance claims by ex-wives because Muslim women could no longer make claims under CrPC Section 125.[5]

Responses to the Bill became largely framed by Congress and conservative Muslim rhetoric emphasising the consti-tutional protection of minority rights to govern their own domestic lives free from state interference and in accord with the (supposed) requirements of their religious beliefs. In opposing the Bill, the Hindu Right also focused on minority rights, but in order to accuse Congress of cynically refusing to intervene in Muslim family law in order to retain the 'Muslim vote bank', and of 'appeasing' Muslims by according them more rights than the majority Hindu population (for instance, by letting Muslim men evade the obligations entailed under CrPC 125); the conservative Muslim stance was viewed as confirmation that Muslim men victimise their womenfolk and that Islam is inherently oppressive to women. Soon, this was explicitly linked to the Hindu Right's increasingly assertive proclamations over the Babari Masjid in Ayodhya and to the wider communalisation of politics, marked by Muslim vulnerability to physical and rhetorical attacks from the Hindu Right and by the electoral successes of the BJP in the 1990s. In terms of subsequent political developments, then, a minority rights and communal politics reading of the Shah Bano case clearly has considerable justification.[6] Indeed, during our research in 1990-91, many Hindu men cited the Shah Bano case as evidence of Hindu victimisation, of Muslim appeasement, and of the justice of the Babari Masjid campaign, whilst Muslim women and men in Bijnor discussed the Shah Bano case in relation to communal politics, not the rights of Muslim women.

Yet the Shah Bano case was certainly not simply about minority rights and communal politics. At its core are crucial issues about women's economic entitlements. Liberal Muslims opposing the Muslim Women Bill asserted that generosity to ex-wives after the 'iddat period would not be contrary to the spirit of Islam or signify that Islam was endangered. Various feminist organisations opposed the Bill because it disadvan-taged Muslim women vis-à-vis other Indian women, attacked the negative comments about Islam in the Supreme Court judgement and highlighted the paltry sums normally awarded in maintenance: Shah Bano herself was granted just Rs179.20 per month by the Supreme Court after a lower court had originally granted her Rs25. Feminists also contested Hindu Right claims that Muslim women were especially disadvan-taged and that the position of Hindu women was unproblematic, and they argued that the furore distracted attention from the inability of Indian women in general to ensure their financial security outside marriage. Such voices, however, became increasingly marginalised in the unfolding debate and by the Hindu Right's interventions.

Gender equity is enshrined in the Indian Constitution – but so too is freedom to practise religion. During the 1980s, the Indian government was swayed in turn by the contradictory demands of Muslim conservatives and the Hindu Right, for whom women were a crucial part of the terrain on which battles about minority rights and national identity were fought.[7] As the Shah Bano case demonstrated, religious freedom may be privileged over gender equity when the two conflict: 'community' self-regulation on matters covered by personal laws is a core element of religious freedom, yet the protection of religious freedom can have an extremely detrimental impact on women's rights (Jeffery 1999; Kapur & Cossman 1995). Accounts of the Shah Bano case, however, were dominated by a focus on high profile political, legal and constitutional issues. Little attention was paid to the implications of the case and of the associated communalisation of politics for communal and gender politics at the grassroots.

Community and Gender in Rural Bijnor

Domestic life in rural Bijnor is premised on some striking commonalities that deny equality of opportunity for males and females, whether Hindu or Muslim, rich or poor. Broadly speaking, kinship and marriage, residence patterns, property ownership and control over resources, and demographic profiles reflect what Dyson and Moore have called the 'northern demographic regime' (Dyson & Moore 1983).[8]

Throughout the region, productive resources, especially land, are owned (albeit inequitably) and managed by men. Women – whether as daughters or as wives – scarcely ever own land or any other substantial economic resources, irrespective of community or social class (Agarwal 1994). A girl normally depends on her father and brothers to meet the costs of raising her and of arranging her marriage. At all levels of the class hierarchy, the most honourable form of marriage requires the bride's parents and their wider kin network to provide a dowry. Villagers regularly complain about the escalation in people's expectations of what will be included in the dowry and fears about dowry harassment are widespread. Providing a dowry can entail major outlays for clothing and jewellery for the bride and members of her husband's family, household goods – bed, bedding, cooking utensils etc. – and, among Hindus, cash. Certainly, parents cannot always achieve this ideal for their daughters and those who fail to save for their daughters' marriages are subject to widespread censure or pity. On the other hand, poor or disabled men often fail to attract a respectable dowry marriage and may have to resort to 'buying a bride' (see below for more on this).

Normally, the newly married woman migrates to her husband's village. Usually, this is accomplished gradually, with increasingly longer periods spent in her in-laws' home inter-spersed with increasingly shorter visits to her natal village. If the mother-in-law is alive, the new bride can expect to spend some years sharing a cooking hearth with her. Since young married women should be deferential, especially to men (and to older women) in their husband's village, the new bride will probably be subject not only to her husband's controls but also to those of his mother for some time after the marriage (Jeffery & Jeffery 1996a). Women's fertility is vitally important to their in-laws, yet the physiological processes associated with fertility and childbearing (sexual intercourse, menstruation, pregnancy, birthing and post-partum bleeding) are matters of shame (sharm kð båt) and/or of pollution (locally termed gandagð). Moreover, Muslims and Hindus alike readily express a preference for sons over daughters, largely grounding their views on parental anxieties about providing dowries for daughters and on the importance of having sons to ensure support in old age (Jeffery et al. 1989). This part of UP – and northern South Asia in general – has long been notable for very masculine sex ratios, attributable to the differential care of young boys and girls, to high rates of maternal mortality, and more recently to sex selective abortions.

Most women are not employed outwith the family enterprise, but are family workers in domestic units where they are subordinated to men and older women. Whilst a young married woman's work may be trivialised by her in-laws (and even by herself), she plays an important economic role in the well-being of her husband's household, cooking, child-rearing, caring for livestock or working in the family fields. Variations in women's work relate primarily to the class position of their husbands' households, but also to life-cycle changes and differences in household composition (rather than religious community). In the wealthiest households, controls over women's mobility beyond domestic space are evidenced in seclusion practices locally known as purdah: the women work almost wholly in and around the home. Somewhat poorer households may endeavour to keep their womenfolk engaged in activities based around the home, generally unpaid work for the household, although some women earn small incomes at home by spinning cotton thread or stitching clothes for neighbours. Women in the poorest households may be compelled to seek employment as domestic servants or field labourers (often only seasonally) for richer households. Poor, and usually elderly, widows (or women with husbands whose earnings are insufficient) may practise as dåðs (traditional birth attendants), a low status occupation associated with pollution (Jeffery et al. 2002; Jeffery & Jeffery 1993a). Fear of sexual harassment, the lack of culturally acceptable job opportunities, and the view that 'eating' women's earnings is shameful for men are all potent disincentives to seeking employment, even for very poor women. In any case, most women in rural Bijnor are not well placed to support themselves: very few have the schooling or training that could enable them to become economically independent.[9]

Marriage migration has important consequences for married women. Unlike her husband, a young married woman generally has little 'social capital', because she is separated from the networks of kin and friends she established during childhood. Nevertheless, her parents and brothers remain concerned for her. Partly, this is reflected in the things they continue to present to her. Indeed, Hindu and Muslim women describe their 'income' (åmdanð) as the foodstuffs (grain, sugar products), jewellery, clothing and cash (and very occasionally livestock) sent by their natal kin after the rice and wheat harvests, at festivals (e.g. Id for Muslims, Holi for Hindus), when they give birth, when their children are married, and when there are marriages and births in their natal household. Usually, however, such gifts are neither regular nor sufficient to furnish all their requirements. Indeed, women whose parents and brothers are financially straitened may receive little or no such 'income'.

Some features of domestic life suggest that many Muslim women may – in some respects – be rather better placed than the typical Hindu woman in rural Bijnor. Hindus arrange their children's marriages beyond the village and usually at some distance (25-30 km was common); women are usually married into households where they know no one and only rarely are two closely related women married into the same village. Muslims generally arrange their children's marriages within a smaller geographical radius (about 3 km or less, and occasionally even within the village). Further, Muslims often arrange marriages between relatives (sometimes even first cousins, who would be prohibited as marriage partners for Hindus). While Hindus accuse Muslims of marrying their 'sisters', Muslims scorn Hindus' propensity to marry their daughters into households of distant strangers. Deceptions about the potential bride's or groom's character or education, or the standing of the family are a source of considerable anxiety.[10] Not entirely implausibly, Muslims claim that their densely knit kinship networks enable Muslim parents to know a lot about a potential groom and his close relatives before agreeing to a marriage. Similarly, Muslims' dense networks permit the effective and rapid communication of information that can enable parents to exert pressure or even ostracise miscreants if their married daughter is mistreated or subject to dowry harassment. It certainly appears that dowry demands and dowry harassment of young married women – the fear of which plagues Hindus – are uncommon among Muslims.

Of course, dense marriage networks do not guarantee a woman's well-being after marriage – but Muslim women are normally less cut off from their natal kin than are Hindu women. Married Hindu women normally receive visits from their brothers, but many never receive visits from their parents (particularly the mother); and they rely on their husband or brothers to accompany them to their natal village for visits – if they have time. Many married Muslim women, though, can walk to their natal village without a male chaperon – although maybe with their children or another married woman – and it is not uncommon even for their mothers to make the reverse trip. Muslim women often claim that they can more easily maintain contact with their natal kin than Hindu women can (although many see this as a rather ambiguous benefit, because parents cannot easily be spared knowledge of their marital troubles).

The issue here, though, is emphatically not whether Muslim women in rural Bijnor are less (or, indeed, more) oppressed than Hindu women. Rather, the above discussion is intended to help us dismantle the claims of the Hindu Right about the 'Muslim woman' and her special vulnerability to 'Islamic tradition'. In terms of control over resources, the labour process and of how males and females are valued, the normal day-to-day functioning of domestic life in rural Bijnor is an important site (though certainly not the only one) for an 'everyday sexism' that transcends the communal boundary. Basically, a married woman – whether Muslim or Hindu – is economically dependent on her husband and his kin: they are responsible for providing for her throughout her life, meeting her daily living expenses for food, clothing, medical care and so forth. Young married women's room for self-determination in their affinal village is severely circumscribed by their lack of economic and social power (Jeffery & Jeffery 1996a: 1-37). Close marriage and lower dowry do not add up to greater autonomy for Muslim women, but they probably do make the negotiation of dependency somewhat easier for them. Few Hindu or Muslim women in rural Bijnor, however, regard their dependency as problematic and many fear the 'responsibility' (zimmedårð) that independence (åzådð) would entail (Jeffery & Jeffery 1994a; 1996b; 1993b). The limitations of women's dependency, however, are starkly exposed by marital breakdown.

Marital Breakdown

Conversations with women in rural Bijnor suggest that marital bliss is somewhat elusive. Women often resent how their husbands, their mothers-in-law and other in-laws treat them. Many women complain that they cannot visit their parents as often as they wish, that they are required to work extremely hard and yet their efforts are inadequately appreciated, or that marital violence is commonplace.

Nevertheless, few marriages end in separation, a term we are using to encompass all cases of marital breakdown, including the minority of formal divorces.[11] Most separations occur in the first few years of a marriage, when there are few, if any, children. Beyond that, though, it is impossible even to hazard rates of marital breakdown. It is a 'shameful matter' (sharm kð båt) and we often learnt of separations or marital difficulties by chance, when querying gaps in women's maternity histories, when old marital conflicts became part of people's weaponry in contemporary disputes, or when young women returned to their natal village and became the focus of gossip. Our most detailed data relate to the key informant couples, among whom 5 women (about 6 per cent) had experienced separation: one Muslim woman and three Hindu women were in second (or later) marriages and another Muslim woman had been 'divorced' by her husband but had returned to live with him. This figure cannot be extended to the populations as a whole, of course; nor can these cases give a reliable indication of which spouse is more likely to initiate the separation or of differential rates of marital breakdown, say by economic position or community. Nevertheless, whilst these cases and the others we learnt about vary in their specifics, there are some common features, whether they occurred before or after the Shah Bano case.

A central element of Hindu Right anti-Muslim rhetoric concerns the 'triple talåq'. The apparent ease with which Muslim men can divorce their wives – by pronouncing talåq three times in one sitting – is regarded as another example of Muslim women's special vulnerability. Allegedly, the triple talåq means that marital breakdown is commonplace amongst Muslims and that Muslim men are routinely repudiating their wives on a capricious whim (by implication, in contrast to Hindu men). But the 'pseudo-champions of Muslim women' may have a communal rather than women's rights agenda in their commentaries on the triple talåq – and they also distract attention from the legal vulnerabilities of Hindu women (Navlakha 1994).[12]

Certainly, the stipulations laid out in theological treatises and in the statute books of the Indian state provide part of the context within which the state and other institutions operate both nationally and locally. Nevertheless, the 'customary' and taken-for-granted procedures by which ordinary people deal with marital breakdown do not necessarily relate closely to them.[13] A focus on the writings of Islamic theologians might lead one to suppose that divorce would be common amongst Muslims, but this is a false trail. In rural Bijnor, marital breakdown is not very common, and nor is it more likely to occur amongst Muslims than Hindus. Indeed, rather than the marked differentiation between Muslims and Hindus that a focus on theology or law might predict, customary responses to marital problems and marriage breakdown demonstrate further parallels. Formal divorce procedures are hardly ever deployed. Few people take marital disputes to secular law courts and Muslim couples are unlikely to take their case to a qåzð. Rather, informal kin- and village-based mechanisms are central, both in trying to prevent marital breakdown and in dealing with it once it happens – amongst Hindus and Muslims alike.

Avoiding Marital Breakdown

Men in rural Bijnor do not lightly or frequently oust their wives from the marital home. The labour intensity of work plus the gender division of labour mean that households need able-bodied adult women just as they need men. Men need wives to bear sons to support them in old age and being a responsible householder is an important part of adult men's identity. That said, a separated man is not usually shunned in his natal village, unless he has a reputation for extreme violence or heavy drinking, and he certainly does not lose his home or his land (if any). A separated man can generally find a second spouse – although parents may be reluctant to marry their daughter to a man with a record of marital breakdown and such men's second wives are generally widowed or separated women.[14] These considerations apply to Muslim and Hindu men alike. Few men of either community initiate a separation; when they do so, it is generally through informal means such as despatching their wife to her natal village or failing to collect her after a visit there. The triple talåq is simply not part of Muslim men's everyday repertoire – any more than secular law courts are of Hindu men's.

Marital breakdown is even less attractive for women than it is for men. It is far more than a 'shameful matter', and the economic as well as social prospects facing separated women help to explain why women often devote considerable energy to avoiding it. Recent discussions emphasising the importance of disaggregating the household and of focusing on intra-household negotiation give some leverage here (Agarwal 1997; Kandiyoti 1988; Kandiyoti 1998; Sen 1990). Sen views households as characterised by 'co-operative conflicts', because members have some interests in common and others that differ. Negotiations over conflicts reflect the parties' perceptions of their interests, contributions to the household and entitlements: the outcomes normally benefit those parties with least to lose in the 'breakdown position' (when the household itself dissolves) because they have the greatest bargaining power. Similarly, Agarwal outlines the differential bargaining power and different 'exit options' of household members. Against Sen, though, she argues that women's failures to strike bargains seemingly in their interests should not be interpreted as acceptance of their situations, for there is evidence aplenty that South Asian women critique their situations. An "overt appearance of compliance" is a "survival strategy" (Agarwal 1997: 24) for women who lack economic power (productive and other resources, independent income) and social capital (social support networks after marriage migration, socially sanctioned and gendered styles of bargaining that put men at an advantage) within the household and beyond – as is typical for rural women in Bijnor. This is similar to Kandiyoti's view of the 'patriarchal bargains' struck when women weigh up the short- and long-term costs and benefits of complying with or resisting their situations. Gender inequalities change through an individual's life-time and the relatively power-less young married woman can anticipate a more powerful position as mother-in-law in later years – provided she toes the line meanwhile (Kandiyoti 1988).[15]

In rural Bijnor, women's 'exit options' often make remaining in an uncongenial marriage seem the least worst option when set beside their likely fate as a separated wom-an. Several key informants and others – Hindu and Muslim alike – presented their marital problems as seemingly offering no realistic option but to endure the difficulties. Take Anisa, for example. After she was widowed, her parents wanted to safeguard her future, so they arranged her marriage to Ahmed. About four years later (in 1991), her situation was miserable, because her in-laws taunted her about her second marriage, beat her, refused to let her visit her parents and insulted her relatives if they visited her. How could she escape this situation? She had virtually no contact with her parents and had little prospect of rescue from that quarter:

> If I didn't think of the children, I'd just die. But then I realise there's no one who would care for my children. They'd end up running from one place to the next being beaten.... My first husband never even slapped me with his four fingers, but this one beats me daily.... On occasion, I've considered taking poison. But then I think about the children. Anyway, the villagers would say it was an unlawful death (Jeffery & Jeffery 1996a: 255).

Generally, it is considered inappropriate for parents to become involved in their daughter's marital problems. Indeed, unhappily married women often say nothing to their parents, because they are ashamed or wish to protect their parents from knowing about troubles from which they should remain aloof, as Kavita's account illustrates. Since before her marriage in the late 1980s, Kavita's husband had been having an affair with his older brother's wife. In order to avoid trouble from the couple, Kavita had adopted a policy of silence – both in her in-laws' home and to her parents:

> The last time I visited my parents, my husband complained to them that I fight with him a lot. So my mother asked me why I fight with him. She told me to remain silent and not interfere with him whatever he might do. But how could I tell my parents about my husband's affair and the beatings? I've never said a thing about it to my father when he visits me here. How could I tell him about such a wicked matter? I couldn't tell my mother either. Even if I got the courage to do so, my mother wouldn't be able to say anything to my father. So what would be the point? (Jeffery & Jeffery 1996a: 230).

Parental interventions considered unwarranted or excessively frequent are roundly criticised and create annoyance among their daughter's in-laws. A married daughter is in 'her own' house and is expected to deal with her own difficulties. Nevertheless, parents often do become involved if they consider their daughter cannot resolve or escape her marital problems without their support – a clear recognition of the young married woman's lack of social and economic power. For instance, when news came one evening in 1990 that Brijpal's daughter had consumed rat poison after a dispute with her husband, Brijpal took a party of his young male relatives to threaten his son-in-law (Jeffery & Jeffery 1996a: 192-6).

Sometimes a woman's parents make considerable efforts to achieve a reconciliation or to make it possible for their daughter to tolerate her lot. Shankar's sister, for instance, was married to a man who spent all his earnings on drink. Shankar and his two brothers provided her with money, grain after each harvest and clothing so that she could remain in her in-laws' village with her children (Jeffery & Jeffery 1996a: 190). Often interventions are occasioned when a daughter visits her parents and refuses to return to her husband's home until her in-laws have been confronted. A violent husband will be admonished and told that his wife would not return to his house until he mended his ways. A man whose father makes unseemly advances or whose mother stirs up trouble – criticising his wife's work, demanding that she bring more goods from her parents, taunting her because she has failed to bear any sons – might be told that his wife will not return until he guarantees good treatment in future.

It is not unusual for a young woman to live in her parents' home for several months while these negotiations and threats take their course: Afsana spent nine months in her parents' home in 1982, Zebunissa was in her parents' home for over a year throughout our fieldwork in 1990-1; Promilla reported staying in her parents' home for about a year in the mid 1970s, while Jayavati was back in her widowed mother's house for much of our 1990-1 fieldwork (Jeffery & Jeffery 1996a: 159-60, 219-23, 178-9, 197-9). The husband and members of his close family may make several visits before the young woman is returned to her marital home.[16] Occasionally, a prominent person from the woman's natal village may mediate: the late Kunwar Satya Vira in Dharmnagri enabled several young women to stand firm in refusing to rejoin their husbands, as in the case of Sudesh's daughter (Jeffery & Jeffery 1996a: 132-3). The pressure on a woman's in-laws may include threats of legal action, but they are rarely implemented: local people fear involvement in the legal process, even when their case is strong, because they believe the police and the judiciary to be corrupt.

Marital Breakdown and Women's Economic Vulnerability

Usually, then, marriages break down only after lengthy periods of discord during which the couple's kin will probably have been involved in trying to avert a separation. Sometimes, though, their efforts fail and the marriage breaks down. Generally, this occurs before the wife has sons of an age to support her. Irrespective of who initiates the separation, the woman must leave the home she has shared with her husband: it is his home, not hers. She cannot even remain in her husband's village. Separated women do not obtain ownership or usufruct rights in their ex-husband's land (or other property), any more than they have rights in the marital home; nor do they receive maintenance payments from their ex-husbands or in-laws. And few women have the education to enable them to enter the labour force on favourable terms.

Muslim women know that Islam provides them with rights to the mahr, a cash settlement by a Muslim man on his wife, which is specified in the marriage contract. Sometimes, the husband should give some or all of the mahr immediately after the marriage. More commonly, the mahr is deferred and the husband is expected to give it only if he initiates divorce; the woman who initiates separation forfeits the mahr. In the event of divorce, the mahr notionally provides the separated woman with economic security. There is no parallel among Hindus, which is perhaps why mahr does not figure in the Hindu Right's anti-Muslim discourse.

Muslim women in rural Bijnor are, however, sceptical about the mahr.[17] Many see little sense in claiming it while living with their husband, since it would be spent on the food and clothing they are already receiving. Even if the mahr were given, moreover, it could not provide long-term economic independence. A quarter of the key informants did not know what their mahr was. Of those who did, just one mentioned a mahr of Rs15,000, another ten mentioned sums between Rs1,000 and Rs8,000, and five said their mahr was the 'mahr Fatimi' comprising 125 silver rupees.[18] For the remaining third, the mahr was less then Rs500 (more than half were under Rs100 and several were just Rs25). Several women say they have already consumed far more than their mahr was worth in their husband's home. Others say that their mahr is the focus of banter: Hashmi (whose mahr is Rs125) said 'My husband laughs and says "How much is the mahr anyway? I can give it whenever I wish!"' while Khurshida told us 'My father-in-law teases my husband, saying "Give Khurshida her Rs25 – it's a very heavy mahr!"'

In any case, one third of the key informants (dispro-por-tionately those with the highest mahr) had 'forgiven' or 'renounced' (mihr mu'åf karna) the mahr, mostly under pressure from their husbands. For instance, when Zubeida was being married to her deceased older sister's husband, the proceedings were delayed for four days because of her step-father's insistence that the mahr be Rs5,000: but Zubeida was forced to renounce the mahr later (Jeffery & Jeffery 1996a: 111-2). Two key informants had forgiven the mahr voluntarily in order not to place their husband in debt, while nearly a quarter could not recall if they had forgiven it or not. The general view was 'But the mahr is only forgiven – who is giving it?' and 'The mahr? Who gives it? They all make you forgive it!' Not one woman had received her mahr, either when her marriage was consummated or later: as one woman put it, 'No one at all gives it. Enough! (bas!) There must be one or two men somewhere in the world who give it!'

Even after divorce, women claim, the mahr is not given. Several women said that people are now 'tying' their sons-in-law with a 'price tag' (raqam, meaning a large mahr) to prevent them from initiating divorce, particularly if the marriage is between non-kin – but they saw little point if wives are compelled to renounce the mahr. Others say divorced and separated women are unlikely to receive the mahr, even when they have not forgiven it: 'But what is the benefit of mahr? If a man is going to leave his wife, he'll do so, no matter how much mahr has been set.' The mahr is sometimes shrouded in uncertainty as well as cynicism:

> I forgave it on the first night. But I've heard that mahr forgiven on the first night is not understood to have been forgiven in law. If it is forgiven a few days after the wedding, then it is considered forgiven. I do not really know. But here in the village, who gives the mahr? They don't give the mahr even if they do give talåq![19]

In rural Bijnor, then, Muslim women are not protected from marital breakdown or from financial insecurity after it by the mahr. A separated woman could not live an independent life on the basis of the mahr – but none of the separated Muslim women we knew had received their mahr in any case. In practice, no woman – whether Muslim or Hindu – is likely to receive financial support from her ex-husband.[20]

In other parts of the world, where women's property rights, agricultural work or educational levels permit economic independence, women may establish female-headed house-holds (Chant 1997). South Asia (and the northern areas in particular), however, seems to be characterised by very low levels of female-headed households. For instance, a young widow may remain in her husband's household (and possibly be married leviratically to her husband's brother), or she may return to her natal kin, who may re-marry her or permit her to remain with them as a widow. Widowhood, though, is a more common experience for older women, who will probably remain in their husband's village. Widows occasionally inherit land, but most do not and they can expect to be supported by their adult sons. In relatively wealthy families with daughters but no sons, the 'in-living son-in-law' (ghar jamåð) who moves to his father-in-law's home and runs the farm is a means of averting a female-headed household. Typically, women who inherit land, either as widows or as daughters, cannot manage or cultivate their farm effectively: women are not permitted to plough (although they do many other agricultural tasks) and their mobility beyond the home is limited. Thus, they normally rely on – and live in a household with – male kin.

Depending on the Natal Kin

A separated woman in rural Bijnor, then, does not normally establish her own household. Separation usually entails returning to her natal kin, at least in the first instance. Her natal kin will probably have been contributing to her material well-being already, but her dowry and the other items presented to her may no longer be accessible. Foodstuffs will have been eaten, cooking utensils may have been requisitioned by her mother-in-law. Clothing may have been worn out or presented to an affinal relative and jewellery sold to pay off a debt or buy medicines, or presented to her husband's sister. Cash may have gone on daily expenses or on large-scale expenditures, such as installing a tubewell or refurbishing her house. Sometimes, a woman's parents threaten reprisals, but there is generally little hope of retrieving even a small portion of the items they presented to her, even if they have not been consumed. Further, the woman who visits her parents and tells them of her marital problems could not carry enough with her – apart from her jewellery perhaps – to support her for more than a few days. Those, such as Dilruba, who feared that their marriage might collapse, might have persuaded their parents to store the foodstuffs and cash they presented rather than sending them to their husband's home:

> For the past two years, I've been leaving the things at my mother's house so that I could buy my own necessities there.... Last Id, for instance, I received 2 kg of sugar, 10 kg of unrefined sugar, 5 kg of rice, and 2 kg of flour. I just brought the sugar and left everything else at my mother's house. When he (Dilshad) divorced me and put me out of the house, I went to my mother's home. I sold some unrefined sugar and rice so that I could buy what I needed. Now I'm returning after six days, and my mother and my brother each gave me 10 kg of wheat. I've left it all in my mother's house. What could I do with it if I brought it here? (Jeffery & Jeffery 1996a: 151)

A few women had stored jewellery in their parents' home, because they suspected their parents-in-law or husband had designs on it – but the woman whose husband fails to collect her from her parents' house is more likely to have nothing salted away. In any case, even Dilruba's forward planning would not provide long-term economic independence.

Basically, a separated woman, whether Muslim or Hindu, faces almost certain penury unless she can persuade her natal kin to support her. Certainly, they are generally the separated woman's best source of support – though not necessarily a very good one. Women whose marriages break down are often blamed for failing to adjust to their in-laws' requirements, for bringing shame on their natal family and for damaging the marriage prospects of their unmarried siblings – unless they can plausibly argue that the whole sorry affair resulted from their in-laws' evilness.

Moreover, once a daughter has been provided with a dowry, she should not make further substantial claims on her parents' property, and certainly not on her father's land (if any). Periodic outlays for gifts to her as a married woman are of a very different order – in quantity and in how they are perceived – from meeting the expenses of a separated woman living permanently in her natal village again. Food, clothing, and medical expenses on a daily basis for her and any children who accompanied her, and possibly educating her children and arranging their marriages, would exceed her parents' and brothers' expectations of their financial obligations. She would be construed not simply as a financial burden, but as wrongfully consuming the entitlements of her brothers, their wives and their children. Her natal kin, then, may provide shelter and support only grudgingly and temporarily.

Dependency in Another Marriage

Even women acting decisively to end unhappy marriages cannot ensure that they retain control over their destiny thereafter. If there is no reconciliation, their natal kin generally made haste to place them in new 'marriages'. Among Hindus, these new unions do not involve full marriage rituals; among Muslims they may, if the woman has been formally divorced. Locally, though, the pair are usually regarded as married and their children are considered legitimate. This outcome, however, does not necessarily offer attractive prospects for either party.

The preferred marriage for men is with a previously unmarried woman whose natal kin provide her with a dowry. The separated woman cannot meet the former criterion – and her natal kin may not meet the latter one at all or to the extent that makes her an attractive match. Sometimes, natal kin put together a modest second dowry, but they are unlikely to have retrieved any items from the first dowry and they may be unable or unwilling to foot another substantial bill. Chet Ram was widowed in the mid 1980s; his second wife had been married to an impotent alcoholic and had spent three years in her natal village after refusing to return to him. A few months after she married Chet Ram, her parents presented him with Rs200, a watch and some cloth (Chet Ram had presented her with no clothes or jewellery at the time of their marriage). Of the separated key informants, however, she was the only one remarried like this: the separated (and sometimes also the widowed) woman is more likely to become a 'bought bride', when her new husband 'takes a bride for a price' (bahø mol lenå), particularly if her brothers or another male go-between organise her second match. In the late 1970s, Taslim (in Jhakri) bought Tahira from his sister's husband who lived in Tahira's natal village. In Dharmnagri, Rohtash paid Rajballa's brothers Rs800 in the late 1970s, while Lalit had obtained seven wives in this fashion, including Lakshmi for whom he paid his cousin (MBS) Rs2000 in about 1980 (Jeffery & Jeffery 1996a: 231-44; Jeffery et al. 1989: 39-41). In 1981 Muni left her violent husband and sheltered in the home of a cousin, whose husband sold her for Rs2,000 to her current husband in Nangal.

This is certainly not an approved method of marrying. Usually the man has been unable to arrange a conventional marriage, because he was widowed and already had children or was considered too old by parents with young marriageable daughters, or because he was deserted by a first wife who accused him of mistreatment, or had some social or physical disability, or was extremely poor. Local gossip always suggests that 'bought brides' are from a lower caste, but there is rarely any firm evidence, since these women are all from many miles away and effectively cut off from their natal kin. The woman herself can expect little or no economic and social support from her natal kin. Bought brides come 'empty handed' (<u>kh</u>ål̆ håth), without a dowry or the other gifts associated with the typical bride. They rarely visit their natal kin or receive visits from them and are very poorly placed to protect themselves, whether from taunting neighbours or marital violence. Yet remarriage is the most likely outcome for the separated woman: in the four study villages, just three women had been separated for several years without being remarried. By contrast, some widows had remained with their natal kin for many years without being pressured into remarriage.

It is hardly surprising that women and their natal kin strive so hard to prevent marital breakdowns. The social and economic prospects for separated women pale in comparison with an approved dowry marriage – perhaps even in the face of considerable discord. The similarity in Muslim and Hindu women's experiences of economic dependency within marriage and economic vulnerability after marital breakdown is a key point here. Contrary to Hindu Right assertions, Hindu women in rural Bijnor are not less vulnerable to being left in penury by their husbands than Muslim women are. The types of problems women report, the efforts they put into achieving reconciliation, their reliance on natal kin and the centrality of kin-based mechanisms for dispute resolution, are common across the board. So, too, are the outcomes when the marriage breaks down: women's lack of entitlements in the ex-husband's household, their temporary reliance on their natal kin, and their probable remarriage in circumstances that may prove no better (and may even be worse) than the first marriage.

Legal Reform and Customary Practice

In the next chapter of this volume, we indicate that ethnic differences are indeed signalled in numerous ways in rural Bijnor. Yet if we focus on micro-level everyday life, a bald proposition that Muslims and Hindus are inherently different flies in the face of social complexity. People's identifications crosscut one another in confusing and conflicting ways and their behaviour – for instance, in regard to gender politics – cannot be neatly glossed as 'Muslim' or 'Hindu'. In other words, there are 'multiple patriarchies' cutting across the boundaries of reified religious communities (Sangari 1995). Nevertheless, much of the discourse surrounding the Shah Bano affair – whether emanating from the Hindu Right, conservative Muslims or the state – played on assumptions that Muslims and Hindus are (or ought to be) essentially different. Moreover, the communalisation of contemporary Indian politics has had severe consequences for the attainment of gender justice. Of the many issues that arise from this, we address the role of legal reform and how feminists can engage with the state here. In the next chapter, we explore the possibilities for the mobilisation of grassroots women around issues of gender equity.

In the early years after 1947, there was widespread optimism that the state would act to protect its citizens and that legislative reforms and government planning could achieve social justice, including for women. The disillusionment already in evidence by the late 1960s was exacerbated by the damning evidence of the gulf between women's constitutional rights and their daily lives, presented in the report of the National Committee on the Status of Women in India in 1974. Other events in the 1970s and 1980s (for instance, the notorious Mathura rape case) left many feminists deeply doubtful about the state's capacity to be an effective and reliable ally for women, not least because agents of the state – whether local policemen, national and state legislators or senior judges – have so often been implicated in actions inimical to women's interests. The stocktaking surrounding the 50th anniversary of Indian independence sparked further analysis among feminists about achievements and failures to date, as well as about strategic priorities in the light not just of communalised politics but also of the economic developments of the 1990s, such as structural adjustment, economic liberalisation and consu-merism (Agnes 1995; Agnihotri & Mazumdar 1995; Butalia 1997-8; Kapur & Cossman 1995; Kapur & Cossman 1996; Sangari 1995).

Throughout these debates, the Uniform Civil Code (UCC) has been a recurrent and contentious theme. The report on the Status of Women in India had addressed the matter in the mid 1970s and advocated a UCC on grounds of gender equity, national integration and secularism (National Committee on the Status of Women 1975:57). Until the Shah Bano case, the replacement of the separate systems of personal law by a single gender-equitable UCC was a central demand of feminists in India. The Hindu Right, however, appropriated the idea of the UCC during the Shah Bano controversy, a move that seriously compromised feminist positions on legal reform. If feminists supported the UCC and opposed the Muslim Women Bill, they would risk being co-opted to the agendas of the Hindu Right and antagonising many Muslims by intervening in community affairs. Not to press for gender-equitable legislation pertaining to family matters, however, could leave unchallenged personal laws that are all premised on gender inequity. Not surprisingly, feminist activists in India remain divided over how to define the key issues and how to campaign for gender equity (Agnes 1999; Mukhopadhyay 1998; Rajan 2003: 1-37, 147-173).

Can feminists tackle gender issues without marginalising other dimensions of inequality (caste, class, community)? Can women rely on reforms coming from within 'communities'? Can or should they rely on the state? Should feminists concentrate on legal reforms – and if so, what form should these take (Anveshi Law Committee 1997; Chhachhi et al. 1998; Gangoli & Solanki 1997; Working Group on Women's Rights 1996)? Should feminists focus on legal provisions within the framework of women's dependency in marriage, maybe pressing for larger maintenance payments (which are notoriously difficult to enforce) or for once-off rights in matrimonial property (which might be easier to enforce, but would not be relevant for women married to poor men) (Agnes 1992; Parashar 1997)? Or does a focus on women's rights to maintenance perpetuate the presumption that women are (or should be) dependent on their husbands? Perhaps, indeed, the focus on the UCC falls into the trap of framing issues of gender equity solely in terms of women's position in the 'private' sphere of the family. Maybe the emphasis should be on enabling women to attain the economic viability outside marriage that would be a better long-term remedy for their disempowering dependency within marriage. The recent unearthing of the National Planning Committee's 1938 Report of the Sub-committee on Woman's Role in Planned Economy has highlighted how this (albeit contradictory) document contained not just recommendations for a UCC but also emphasised women's role as productive citizens, whose work would both give them economic rights and benefit the nation (Banerjee 1998; Chaudhuri 1996; Kasturi 1996). Yet government policy since 1947 has been largely oriented to women as members of families, as mothers and as family planning and welfare targets, not as individual citizens and workers. So, should feminist activism also try to improve state policies on employment and training?

Then again, beyond questions about which emphases are most appropriate in relation to government policy and legislation, are feminist activities best focused on the state, given its history of failures? Some feminists do indeed advocate disengagement from the state because of this. Others object to the state's totalising and modernising agenda. In our view, though, disengaging from the state would leave carte blanche to pressure groups unlikely to have women's interests at heart. Further, at the very least, the law plays important symbolic and normative roles in stipulating what is permissible or intolerable. Gender discriminatory legislation should have no place on the statute books and it is vital that the many gender (and other) inequities still enshrined in the legal system be removed. Nevertheless, it is crucial to ask how the law operates at the grassroots and thus how much priority and energy should be focused on legislative reforms and on the state at the centre. Even when the framing of legislation apparently points towards the eradication of gender inequities, implementation that is itself gender-biased may undermine the legislation's intent and prevent women from ensuring that their legal rights are met in practice.

Marital breakdown in rural Bijnor is just one such case in point. Prior to the Muslim Women (Protection of Rights on Divorce) Act, Hindu and Muslim women alike had no customary right to maintenance after marital breakdown and they relied on support from their natal kin or from a new husband. None of the separated Muslim women we knew had received the mahr or even approached a qåzð in search of support in enforcing their claims. Few women, whether Hindu or Muslim, could have afforded to employ lawyers and make maintenance claims under CrPC Section 125; after all, Shah Bano herself exercised control over no funds and she could pursue her claims in the courts only because of financial support from her adult sons. The CrPC Section 125 played a very limited role in preventing women from becoming destitute after marital breakdown. And, in practice, the Muslim Women Act has had no observable impact on the economic situation of Muslim women in rural Bijnor. Nor did the Act differentiate the economic positions of Hindu and Muslim women in practice. (The wider impact of the Shah Bano affair on local communal politics should not be under-estimated, however.) Briefly,

Muslim and Hindu women's economic insecurity in the event of marital breakdown has remained comparable.

In other words, what practical effects would a gender-equitable UCC – or indeed other legislation focusing on gender issues – have on most ordinary rural Indian women's experiences of family life? Even in a situation of formal legal gender equality, there is no guarantee that substantive gender equality would result, without interventions in local-level social, economic and political processes beyond the legal domain – such as gender inequalities in access to property, income and entitlements in everyday practice. In rural Bijnor, there already is a (fairly) 'uniform customary code' with respect to gender politics at the domestic level, one that offers little protection to women, especially young women. Many feminists would argue that empowering and mobilising women is the most effective remedy for this sort of issue (see, for instance, Molyneux 1998; Moser 1989; Rajan 2003). As we argue in the next chapter, however, this would be difficult in rural Bijnor.

The Shah Bano case certainly had a momentous impact on India's recent political history: the constitutional dilemmas it raised are unresolved and the scars of communal disturbances remain. Yet discussion of the case has mostly focused on the state at the centre, on the formal legal realm, and on the implications of the case for communal politics. All this has tended to divert attention away from the need to tackle gender politics at the grassroots and across the communal divide. Rights and obligations during marriage and after marital breakdown are not narrow legal matters amenable to simple legal resolution: they are intensely political issues. Customary procedures for dispute resolution reflect power imbalances at the micro-level. Crucially, most rural women in north India – whether Hindu or Muslim – currently lack entitlements to economic resources and they are relatively powerless in the domestic arena and beyond. Without far-reaching changes at that level, women's formal legal rights are likely to remain a dead letter.

Notes

[1]　The British also codified vocabularies and grammars of local languages, systematised place names and engaged in extensive geographical and geological surveys. For more on this see, for example, Appadurai (1993); Cohn (1987); Ludden (1993); Pandey (1990).

[2]　The state's non-involvement in the 'private sphere' was (and still is) notional, of course. Prior to 1947, several instances of state involvement generated widespread debate and opposition: on sati (widow immolation) and the age of consent see Mani (1989; 1990); Parashar (1992); Rajan (2003); Sangari (1995); Sarkar (1993).

[3]　In Pakistan, by contrast, revised legislation passed in 1961 as the Muslim Family Laws Ordinance attempted to enhance the legal rights of Muslim women by reducing some of the most overtly discriminatory provisions of the 1937 Shariat legislation. Implementation and enforcement, however, have remained partial at best: see, for instance, Chipp-Kraushaar (1981); Mumtaz & Shaheed (1987: 57-59).

[4]　The following provide useful accounts of the case: Chhachhi (1991); Engineer (1987); Z. Hasan (1989; 1993; 1994; 1999); Kishwar (1986); Kumar (1993: 160-171); Mody (1987); Palriwala & Agnihotri (1996: 511-519); Pathak & Rajan (1989). The case raised many issues, including (for Muslims) state intrusion into the 'private' sphere of religious minorities (that is echoed in Muslims' responses to the family planning programme) and (for the Hindu Right) the trope of the Muslim woman as victim (that also comes up in relation to polygamy); see Chapter 1 and Chapter 3 for more on these points.

[5]　Certainly, the most widespread interpretation at the time was that Muslim women's rights were being undermined. Subsequently,

however, the Act's requirement that a Muslim man provide his ex-wife with 'fair and reasonable provision' has given space for some legal decisions in which Muslim women obtained sizable lump sum payments, a situation that was ratified by a Constitutional Bench in 2001. For more on this, see Agnes (1992; 1996; 1999); Engineer (1999); Menski (2001: 231-294); Mitra & Fischer (2002); Mukhopadhyay (1994, 1998).

6   See Chapter 1, note 2 for references on the Ayodhya affair and the communalisation of politics.

7   Literature on this topic addresses how women are iconised in relation to the nation or community, the role of women activists in the Hindu Right, and how organisations of politicised religion advocate conventional family roles for women, argue for the importance of personal law in 'defining' community, and use gendered stereotypes in communal politics: see Bacchetta (1993; 1994; 1996); Basu (1993; 1995; 1999); Z. Hasan 1989; 1993; 1994; 1999); Jeffery & Basu (1999); Kandiyoti (1991); Sarkar (1991); Sarkar & Butalia (1995). The complex interplay between gender and national or ethnic identities is not an issue unique to India: see, for instance, Anthias & Yuval-Davis (1992); Moghadam (1994a; 1994b); Yuval-Davis (1997).

8   For more on the position of women in north India more generally, see Agarwal (1994); Chowdhry (1994); Dyson & Moore (1983); Mandelbaum (1986, 1988); Raheja (1988, 1995); Raheja & Gold (1994); Sharma (1980); Wadley (1994).

9   According to the 2001 census of India, the rural literacy rate in Bijnor for females aged seven and above was 44.6 per cent (the urban rate was 55.5 per cent) (Census of India 2001 data supplied in electronic format File ST2001RU, Table 1).

10   One of our research assistants (a Brahman woman) said that several recent marriages in her extended family had breached conventional prohibitions on marriages between certain relatives precisely because of the anxiety about the deceptions perpetrated by strangers.

11   We are leaving widowhood on one side here. Widowhood does not necessarily reflect acrimony between husband and wife (and possibly wider kin) and the consequences of widowhood are also normally somewhat different from separation/divorce. For more on widowhood, see Chen (1998); Chen & Drèze (1992; 1995a; 1995b); Chowdhry (1994: 74-120, 356-377); Jeffery & Jeffery (1996a: 231-

73); Kolenda (1987a; 1987b: 288-354); Vatuk (1990; 1995); Wadley (1994: 25-9, 154-162; 1995a; 1995b).

[12] The recurrent and acrimonious discussions in the All India Muslim Personal Law Board highlight the diverse opinions of experts in Islamic Law on whether the triple talåq is desirable or even permissible.

[13] Among other things, the papers in Ahmad (2003) indicate the diverse legal and extra-legal procedures adopted by Muslims in India. The paper by Rafat (2003) deals with Muslims in Bijnor town and many of the points she makes echo those that we are making here.

[14] It is somewhat problematic to use the term 'marriage' for such second unions since they would rarely meet formal legal definitions of marriage, even though local people generally regard them as 'marriages'. See below, for a discussion of the second marriage from the woman's viewpoint.

[15] Agarwal (1997) and Kandiyoti (1998) also both address 'rationality' and the extent to which women understand the bases of their subordination or are submerged in false consciousness.

[16] If the problem is disputes with the husband's parents or brothers and their wives, both the woman and her husband may live in her natal village to preserve their relationship, e.g. Mamta and her daughter Rani (Jeffery & Jeffery 1996a: 224-6).

[17] This account is based on discussions with our Muslim key informants as well as many other Muslim men and women in rural Bijnor.

[18] This is the mahr specified when Fatima, the daughter of the Prophet Muhammed, was married; it is sometimes called sharia mahr. Silver rupees are more valuable than contemporary coins of the same face value.

[19] It seems to be common for Muslim women not to receive their due according to Islamic law. Other accounts of contemporary practices with respect to mahr in India include Agarwal (1994: 227-8, 260); Agnes (1996); Ahmed-Ghosh (1994: 178-80); Engineer (1992: 111-13); Husain (1976: 119-37, 193-94); Jacobson (1976: 185, 207; 1995: 187); Jeffery (2000: 57-9); Mann (1992: 69; 1994: 154-156); Papanek (1982: 24-5); Rafat (2003: 89ff.); Singh (1992: 81). For historical sources see Ali (1832: Vol. 1, 345); Blunt (1969:198); Crooke (1921: 75); Kozlowski (1989); Metcalf (1990: 139-42).

[20] We can note the irony of conservative Muslim claims to orthodoxy over the issue of maintenance of ex-wives during the Shah Bano controversy, since Muslim women commonly do not receive financial entitlements – such as mahr and inheritance – over which there does not seem to be doctrinal dispute.

ENGENDERING COMMUNALISM

EVERYDAY AND INSTITUTIONAL ASPECTS OF GENDER AND COMMUNITY

In Chapter 2, we argued that, compared to Hindu women, Muslim women in rural Bijnor are not rendered especially vulnerable by Islamic tradition or by how they are treated by Muslim men. Rather, Hindu and Muslim women are embedded in broadly comparable systems of gender politics at the household level – most notably their lack of economic and social power. Moreover, Hindu and Muslim women themselves not only noted the parallels but developed critical commentaries – which raises the question: might rural women be able to mobilise to combat what we have called 'everyday sexism'?

Whilst religious doctrines play only a rather oblique part in these parallels in women's domestic lives, we should not be tempted to conclude that women' religious affiliations are irrelevant, however. This chapter focuses on the social and political significance of 'religious' community membership. As we noted in Chapter 1, rural Muslims and Hindus in comparable class and caste positions are differentiated from one another in terms of some health, education and demographic indicators. Here, we explore the reasons behind this. We argue that Muslim women – as members of a religious minority – are more adversely affected than Hindu women by communalised social and political processes that operate beyond the domestic arena at the local level.

Everyday Sexism and Rural Women's Critiques

Women from Dharmnagri and Jhakri often visited us after consulting one of the staff at the Dharmnagri government dispensary where we lived. Thus, we often overheard and participated in conversations between Hindu and Muslim women who would otherwise have had little occasion to meet. One day in 1982, Najma and Khurshida (two Muslim women), Viramvati and Vimla (two Scheduled Caste women) and the Muslim woman who was then the assistant to the Auxiliary-Nurse Midwife (ANM) congregated in our residence. Conversation turned to women's clothing. In rural Bijnor, married Hindu women wear a dhotð (like a cotton sårð) with a kurtå (a long-sleeved shirt with the bodice down to the hips). Married Muslim women wear shalwår or pajåmå (cotton trousers with wide or narrow legs) and qamðz (a long-sleeved dress down to the knees). Vimla looked Najma and Khurshida up and down with a mischievous glint in her eye. 'With a dhotð' she commented to Najma, 'we can easily pee when we need to, but you have to untie your pajåmå cord and pull your pajåmå down.

What happens if a man comes along suddenly? Surely it must be hard to get up quickly. We can just stand up and he won't see anything!' The others laughed uproariously. 'True,' replied Najma, 'But our pajåmå cords make it harder for our husbands to trouble us [demand sex]! With your dhotð, how can you keep him off you?' Vimla and Viramvati nodded assent and more raucous laughter broke out. Once it quelled, the ANM's assistant broke in – still giggling as she did so: 'And anyway, Muslim courtyards generally have dry latrines, so we Muslim women don't have to contend with our pajåmås in the open space of the fields like you Hindu women do!'[1]

The above interchange suggests an ignorance of some intimate details of domestic life that would easily have been evident if these women visited one another's homes. In addition, though, it highlights some common idioms and assumptions about women and men, about female bodily modesty and the embarrassment of being spied less than fully clad by a man, and about sexual relations between husbands and wives. Indeed, Hindu and Muslim women alike often provide distinctly critical commentaries on aspects of 'everyday sexism' – commentaries that assume that women on both sides of the communal divide face similar difficulties and dilemmas in their daily domestic lives. They raise issues about marriage arrangement and dowry harassment. They hold forth about the difficulties that parents face in trying to protect their married daughters. Women freely proffer advice to one another on how to deal with medical symptoms and recalcitrant daughters-in-law. Sometimes, mixed groups of women lament that men's quick tempers make women liable to frequent beatings, and insist that all married women in the locality have experienced marital violence personally. Or they complain about how their husbands and mothers-in-law disregard their illnesses or appreciate their work so little. A non-literate woman may engage in self-deprecation, lamenting her inability to read in the same terms as an uneducated man: that they are 'a thumbprint person', 'a blind person' or 'like a beast'. And, sometimes, women gleefully recount how they manage to circumvent their mother-in-law's commands, or succeed in persuading their parents to chastise their husbands. Wedding songs and songs to mark a boy's birth are other means by which women – Muslim and Hindu alike – humorously critique domestic authorities, husbands or mothers-in-law (Jeffery & Jeffery 1996a; Jeffery et al. 1989; Raheja & Gold 1994).

In these and other ways, village women readily critique at least some aspects of their domestic situations. Behind Vimla and Najma's jesting and banter, then, was there a potential for sisterhood transcending the communal boundary? Could songs act as catalysts for empathy between Muslim and Hindu women? Could these critiques and resistances provide a focus for a gender-based mass activism of rural women? Could women's grievances create an effective rallying cry for women to identify primarily as women across the communal boundary? For several reasons, we think not.

For one thing, many aspects of everyday family life and gender differences are so 'naturalised' that the critical reach of women's complaints is rather limited. In practice, women's critiques are equivocal and co-exist with endorsements of substantial elements of the status quo. Distant marriage, for instance, is resented because a woman cannot easily maintain contact with her natal kin. But women do not question the propriety of marriage migration as such, even though it seriously disempowers a young married woman in her husband's household. Women rarely consider their lack of land rights and their dependence on their in-laws problematic, yet they are outraged by harassment of brides over their dowries. The efforts people put into preventing marital breakdown reflect most women's lack of realistic options beyond dependency within the household. Few women are likely to mount far-reaching challenges to their best source of support and wellbeing – albeit not always a very good source, and one that is often experienced as a source of misery too. Women moan about frequent childbearing, which they see as debilitating (or even life threatening) for themselves and their children, as well as likely to create financial difficulties in future. They often complain about their difficulties in obtaining contraceptives (and many requested medical and contraceptive advice from us rather than from government health staff). Yet they do not challenge local preferences for sons and they commiserate with women with several daughters or no children at all.

Women's complaints also jostle with critical and unsupportive behaviour towards other women. Women expostulate about how men devalue their work – and about women's inability to co-operate over sharing household tasks. Critical commentaries on marital violence are often tempered by assertions that men should not tolerate wilful and defiant wives. Pride in women's capacity to work hard and to endure the pains of childbirth co-exists with endorsing negative and shameful images in relation to re-productive physiology – such as menstrual and childbirth pollution – and such self-deprecation severely hampers the forging of allegiances to one another as women. In any case, far from necessarily having interests in common, women within a single household – leave aside beyond – may have divergent interests and conflicting loyalties. The continual re-positioning of individual women (as daughter, sister, mother or wife) and the shifts in women's perspectives and concerns in the course of the life-cycle mean that women do not speak in unison and that their perspectives are unstable, inconsistent and contradictory. The balance of power in the household is such that rebellion does not necessarily appear a wise course. Older women are often in authority over others. Younger women compete for scarce household resources. Married women's heavy workloads limit their time and energy and their lack of social and economic pow-er puts them into weak positions in the wider community, making it difficult for them either to mobilise support from outside the household or to withstand the backlash if they step out of line. Women's critiques generally translate into individualistic, sporadic and often secretive forms of re-sistance typical of the 'weapons of the weak' (Scott 1985).

Beyond the household, the workplace might indeed be crucial for building women's collective identity and a 'space for participation in civic affairs' (Sunder Rajan 2003:172), but as she herself concedes, the workplace is a 'meager and compromised space' (Sunder Rajan 2003: 173). Certainly, in rural Bijnor, relatively few women are employed outside the home or their household's landhold-ings. Such women are poor (and usually lower caste) and carry out domestic or seasonal agricultural work for richer households. They are often employed in ones or twos, rather than in larger groups. Such work draws attention to women as employers and employees, exposing their divergent interests: women are embedded in households differentially placed in local structures of inequality, which undermines rather than provides bases for wider solidarity. On these grounds alone, the prospects of women's mobilisation around gender issues seem bleak. Most crucial for our discussion here, however, are the implications of women's affiliations to different religious communities.

Communalism in Bijnor

Residents of Bijnor District pride themselves that it is an area notable for its 'communal harmony'. Bijnor (people claim) experienced no serious communal problems even during the Partition period. And there were apparently no major outbreaks of communal violence in the district during the 1980s, in contrast to the neighbouring districts of Meerut and Moradabad.

Nevertheless, the Shah Bano case and, more directly, the Babari Masjid campaign had impacts in Bijnor (Basu 1995c; Jeffery & Jeffery 1994b). In September 1990, attempts were made to build a temple on disputed land next to a mosque in Bijnor town itself, an uncanny parallel with the unfolding events in Ayodhya. Muslim and Scheduled Caste people travelling to Bijnor for an 'anti-communalism' rally held by the then UP Chief Minister, Mulayam Singh Yadav, were involved in fighting in the villages they passed through. Hindu kar sevaks (volunteers) on their way to Ayodhya were imprisoned in the girl's secondary school in Bijnor town. On October 30 1990, Hindu activists made the first (unsuccessful) attempt to demolish the Babari Masjid in Ayodhya. In Bijnor, women from local branches of the Durgå Vahðnð (Durga's Army, the women's wing of Vishwa Hindu Parishad) led a 'victory procession' through the streets to mark the day's events in Ayodhya, allegedly chanting slogans such as 'Hindu Råm kå bacchå, Musalmån haråm kå bacchå' (Hindus are Ram's children, Muslims are bastards). Many parts of the district (including rural areas) were convulsed by violence, murder, theft and arson, and a curfew was in force in Bijnor town for over a week.

In 'normal' times, women in rural Bijnor are affected by controls over their mobility and demeanour in the world beyond their homes. In a communally charged climate, however, women's vulnerability is likely to become especially overt (Basu 1993; Chakravarti et al. 1992; Das 1990; Mann 1994; Moghadam 1994b; Sarkar 1993; Sarkar 1991). In 1990, women were among the early victims of police firing in Bijnor town. Local police and the Provincial Armed Constabulary (PAC) were said to have attacked Muslim women. Allegations and rumours spread like wildfire into the surrounding rural areas – of harassment, abductions, and rapes, of Hindu men goring the pelvic regions of Muslim women with trishul (tridents), of Muslim men amputating the breasts of Hindu women, and of women whose relatives had all been killed and who had been reduced to begging in the hinterland villages. Muslim women going to the post-graduate women's college in Bijnor were said to have been challenged to respond 'Ram Ram' to Hindu youths from the senior secondary school next door, or to have their way barred.

Muslims certainly believed that the civil disorder had borne particularly heavily on Muslim women and that fears for their safety might result in the more strenuous application of restraints on their access to public space. The widespread sense that 'the times are bad' and that girls and women are particularly vulnerable seriously compromises the access of women and girls to education and health care, whether state or not. Fear of assault might make parents loath to let their daughters attend school or make some get their daughters married at an earlier age than they might otherwise have intended – which would mean earlier starts to childbearing careers. And if sick women, or women with sick children, need to be more carefully chaperoned than before, visits to a clinic or urban hospital are likely to be delayed. Indeed, during the curfew in Bijnor town, attendance at the Dharmnagri clinic by local Muslim women declined sharply because young men from nearby were reputed to be preparing sharpened bamboo staves in readiness to attack any Muslims within range. During the 1991 general election campaign, too, Hindu assertiveness intimidated Muslims, and Muslim women in Jhakri said that they would be too frightened to cast their vote at the polling booth in Dharmnagri.

The viciousness of the arson and killing in Bijnor town and its hinterland apparently took many locals by surprise. Communal disturbances are usually urban phenomena, often described as dramatic disruptions of a basically non-communalised (though not necessarily non-violent) order sparked off by outside agents provocateurs. In Bijnor, many preferred this kind of reading (Jeffery & Jeffery 1994). Indeed, outsiders certainly were involved. As in other instances, the breakdown in public order in Bijnor was less a matter of a 'riot' than of systematic attacks against Muslims and their property. Moreover, agents of the local state – the police, the PAC, District Magistrates and the Army – engaged in gendered and communally biased repression in the course of restoring order (Das 1990; Engineer 1984; Saberwal & Hasan 1984).

Focusing on crises and law-and-order, however, underplays what happens between one crisis and the next and deflects attention from long-standing and mundane local processes that provide a fertile soil for communalism and are the context for (and may be influential in giving rise to) periodic turmoil (Brass 2002). Communalism, in other words, is not just a matter of high profile national politics or dramatic events that result in violent death or serious bodily injury. Nor is it merely episodic. If we focus only on the violent and tragic aspects of communalism – the 'riots' and disturbances that erupt in times of crisis – we ignore the grinding and routinised aspects of communalism that pervade people's lives on a daily basis, in ways, moreover, that are deeply gendered. At the local level, and often in matters of everyday significance, gender politics and communal politics were intertwined with one another, despite the lack of overt communal tension that seemingly characterised Bijnor society. During our 1982-83 fieldwork in Bijnor, communal identities did not usually outweigh other sources of identity, and people often voiced countervailing – though somewhat trite – rhetorics about people's common humanity. Nevertheless, the marking of communal difference was an important and well-established feature of rural social life even then, whether 'everyday communalism' (or 'banal' communalism, cf. Billig 1995), or the 'institutional communalism' that structures rural life on a daily basis and affects minorities' access to key resources. Overt expressions of anti-Muslim sentiments may now be more 'permissible' than before 1990, but they are certainly not new, and, in rural Bijnor, such long-standing attitudes have been especially detrimental to Muslim women.

Everyday Communalism

Throughout our Bijnor fieldwork, we have had to engage with the interplay of religious affiliations and communal politics with gender issues. Communal stereotypes have always provided an important means by which people located themselves and others (including us) in the local social topography.

Differences in religious practice certainly provide some ready-made repertoires through which people can differentiate themselves from others. Some Hindus see Muslims as rigid fanatics, and consider Hinduism superior because it accommodates a range of views and deities. But hardly any adults from Dharmnagri attend the local mandir except during major festivals. In the early 1980s, kathå performances were unknown in the village (and they are still not common), and homes in Dharmnagri do not have domestic shrines that are the focus of regular pujå. Few women or men can read the sacred texts of Hinduism, and worship is not a regular part of their daily lives. Indeed, at several domestic festivals we attended, women curtailed the proceedings with comments like, 'enough, that's all I can remember'. Similarly, some Muslims deride Hindus for 'setting up a stone anywhere and worshipping it', and they assert the superiority of Islam and Christianity as monotheistic religions of the Book. But few people in Jhakri can read the Qur'ån Sharðf. A handful have been to Sufi shrines in other parts of UP and one man has been on Hajj to Mecca. Some Muslim men (but by no means the majority) pray regularly at home or in the village mosque. Many women do not know how to recite their prayers – whilst those who do so say that they cannot pray regularly because their work (dealing with animal dung and small children's excrement) precludes the requisite ablutions.

People's sense of identity as a Hindu or as a Muslim, then, derives not so much from daily ritual practices as from a more diffuse awareness of difference. In questioning us about our own practices, people regularly point to contrasts between Hindus and Muslims – how births are marked, how marriages are arranged and what is done with dead bodies. People comment on differences in diet: Hindus characterise Muslims who share a common plate as eating juthå (polluted) food, while Muslims consider that the rigid separation of food onto individual dishes signals a lack of love between family members and friends. Some caste Hindus (in particular) were upset because we accepted food from all those who invited us into their homes, including Scheduled Castes and Muslims, whom they regarded as having dirty habits.

Moreover, as is commonly the case, women in rural Bijnor have been both passive and active markers of communal difference. This is evidenced, for instance, in the taken-for-granted and entirely uncontroversial (at village level at least) way in which marriages are arranged: sexual relationships should take place only within marriage and young people's parents or guardians should arrange their marriages. In normal circumstances, the selection of marriage partners is premised on remaining within caste and community boundaries. People do not knowingly arrange marriages with someone from another caste or community. And married women – the couple's married sisters or aunts, for instance – may play important active roles in this by activating their kinship networks in other villages. Then again, casting slurs on women's reputations or subjecting them to sexual harassment are idioms through which men jockey for position, with those from dominant castes, classes or communities displaying their ability to harass and humiliate women from weaker groups, and those from subordinate groups trying to turn the tables on their superiors. Social controls over women's mobility and general demeanour reflect concerns to protect family honour from such challenges. Nevertheless pre-marital and extra-marital liaisons do sometimes happen: those within castes generally cause only brief scandals, whilst cross-caste relationships are usually harder to handle. Sexual liaisons across the communal boundaries, however, seriously menace the normal social order and may result in violence unless a crisis can be averted.

In the early 1980s, people generally expressed their views in the absence of the 'Other' to whom reference was being made. Interactions across the communal boundary were usually dealt with in a mutually courteous or jovial fashion. The verbalisation of communal stereotypes in the early 1980s was rarely associated with overtly hostile, let alone violent, interactions – although there was clearly that potential. In July 1982, for instance, the exact temporal coincidence of Id-ul-Fitr (at the end of Ramzan) and the Teej festival caused a great deal of good-humoured comment at our vain efforts to cover both events ethnographically.[2] But in April 1991, people were anxious about what trouble might erupt during the near coincidence of Id and Holi, made worse by the imminent elections.[3] The District Magistrate was rumoured to have denied any responsibility for the safety of women on the streets during this period. Conversation was far more likely than before to turn to communal stereotypes and communal politics. The tone of our discussions and the details of people's communal stereotypes had also modulated. From both sides of the communal divide, we sensed levels of anxiety and fear for personal security that had not been overt (or maybe not even been present) previously.

By 1990-91, some of the rhetorics and stereotypes common before the Shah Bano and Ayodhya affairs had been supplanted, or else supplemented, seemingly by commentary emanating from prominent Muslim clerics or from the Hindu Right. Muslims were fearful of upper caste Hindu domination of the police and the PAC, and they worried that the BJP's view of ekta (unity) could only mean the obliteration of Islamic culture and religion. On the other hand, members of the dominant Hindu castes (especially Jats) voiced virulently anti-Muslim sentiments, though members of the 'little' castes often tried to dissociate themselves from this. Jats, for instance, repeatedly reproduced arguments found in the newspapers Dainik Jagran and Amar Ujålå about the determination of present-day Muslims to destroy India like Babur had destroyed Hindu shrines. They complained about the introduction of the

Prophet Muhammad's birthday onto the national calendar and about processions of local Muslims. They said they were justified in taking the law into their own hands to defend themselves and Lord Ram in the face of violent and hot-blooded Muslims who were armed to the teeth. And they welcomed the PAC onslaught on local Muslims.

Since 1990, there has been an increasing presence of the Tablighi Jama'at in the rural areas. This Islamic missionary organisation emphasises the importance of the regular recitation of prayers and other Islamic religious activities, as well as advocating the purging of supposedly Hindu accretions, such as dowry (Metcalf 1999). As has often been the case, disreputable facets of 'women's culture' such as songs, have been a particular target (Banerjee 1989; Gardner 1999; Minault 1994). Similarly, since 2000 or so, busloads of Dharmnagri residents have begun travelling periodically to hear the preaching of a guru who demands austere and moral living of his devotees, although few of his followers in Dharmnagri seem to engage in daily ritual observances. At the same time, there is a small but active cell of the Rashtriya Swayamsevak Sangh (RSS) in a village that abuts Dharmnagri. For the most part, though, there is calm, at least on the surface.

The events of 1990 are an important reference point, however, and developments in the 1990s have served as continual reminders that being a member of a religious minority is a salient aspect of people's identity. Interpretations of the activities of separatist Muslims in Kashmir, the destruction of the World Trade Centre in September 2001, and the attack on the Indian parliament in December 2001 have been characterised by a politically-motivated

Hindu Right rhetoric that demonises Muslims and fuels commonsense stereotypes of Muslims as violent and destructive elements in Indian society. Yet the evidence of numerous reports continues to indicate that Muslims have been the greatest victims of communal violence in terms of loss of life as well as property. The anti-Muslim pogroms in Gujarat in 2002 are an extreme and horrific example of the more general vulnerability of Indian Muslims (Varadarajan 2002). Muslims in Bijnor, as elsewhere in India, now have a heightened awareness of the narrow line between the normal social order and one in which their insecurity is writ large. The normal social order, however, is far from free of communalism – and not just in the sense of everyday communalism.

Local State, Market, and Gendered Institutional Communalism

Processes inherent in the normal workings of the state and in many economic transactions systematically affect the life chances of religious minorities and women. In many arenas, discrimi-nation can certainly be found in the overt and intentionally discriminatory acts of prejudiced individuals. In addition, and perhaps more insidiously, however, normal institutional procedures often perpetuate or result in structured inequalities. People's distribution in job or housing markets, for instance, may be dramatically skewed by discrimination that does not necessarily reflect the intentions of prejudiced individuals. Rather, institutions may operate according to apparently neutral rules and procedures, yet the outcomes of their actions can dramatically signal inequality of opportunity.

The concept of 'institutional racism' was first used in the civil rights movement in the US and later borrowed – as 'institutional sexism' – by the women's movement. Generally, the institutions encompassed are public ones, including businesses and the state. Although these terms have several interpretations, they all connote indirect discriminatory practices that are hard to diagnose, root out or legislate against because they are taken-for-granted and all-pervasive (Rex 1986: 108-118). Here, we use the notion of 'gendered institutional communalism' to encompass similar phenomena in India. These processes are deeply embedded in the normal and apparently gender- and community-neutral everyday workings of many social institutions (such as the state and markets operating at the local level), and they result in outcomes that are systematically biased.

Many writers doubt that the Indian state can be an effective protector of citizens' rights. Considerable uncertainty exists over what minorities – whether women or other disadvantaged groups – can reasonably expect from state action ostensibly on their behalf, or on behalf of 'the general population'. Certainly, the state may sometimes be responsive to popular pressure to introduce legislative and policy reform or to provide vital social services. States, however, are usually controlled by dominant sectors of the population and are rarely neutral arbiters of all their citizens' rights. They may abuse the rights of some or all of their citizens and endorse rather than undermine inequalities. They may act to control the populace, even in the course of providing social services. Further, state institutions react to diverse pressures and we should not imagine that the state acts in unison from a central point in pursuit of a single set of goals. Different state sectors (law and order, social and economic development) cannot be assumed to act in harmony with one another. For instance, much national and state government policy in India – such as agriculture and health – is framed in apparently secular and class- and gender-neutral terms (although we cannot assume that policy-makers intended the disinterested application of policy), whilst the different systems of personal or family law are conspicuously discriminatory on both communal and gender counts.

In any case, the state at the local level is not simply a microcosm of the national state. Despite claims to national uniformity, there is some local discretion in policy formulation and implementation, and attempts to increase decentralisation are regularly announced (and equally often mostly ignored in practice). Local discretion and a lack of adequate monitoring, however, do allow space for a mismatch between pronounce-ments from the centre and normal procedures. National policies – whether seemingly 'neutral' in relation to gender and community or not – are experienced in people's everyday lives only after being mediated through local state institutions, which are marked by gender and community (as well as class and caste) inequalities. Central or State governments promise far more than the local state functionaries will ever deliver. The outcomes often belie national level proclamations of equal opportunities by being systematically (if maybe uninten-tionally) biased, and by acting to sustain (rather than challenge) local systems of inequality.

Until recently, the daily workings of local state institutions have not attracted much attention or been analysed with the same sophistication as the Indian national state (as in Bardhan 1984; Vanaik 1990). Discussions of state involvement in communalism and gender issues have tended to concentrate on legislation and policy-making, and the attempts of the state at the centre to buy off fundamentalist or communalist pressures (Chhachhi 1989; 1991; 1994; Hasan 1994; 1999: for similar material on Pakistan and Bangladesh see Jalal 1991; Kabeer 1991; Mumtaz 1994; Mumtaz & Shaheed 1987). But the varied and rapidly expanding body of ethnographic work now being conducted in dispersed sites of state activity is challenging the 'master concept' of the state as the sole or best route to more sophisticated theorising about its nature in contemporary India (Khilnani 1997). Rather than appearing as a unified actor, the state becomes visible as a range of actors and activities in pursuit of different and often conflicting ends. Such diverse and routine manifestations of state activity as anganwaḍò workers (who run crèches and feeding schemes for young children), land registry officers, District Commissioners and health extension and hospital workers (Gupta 1993; Véron et al. 2003) begin to expose "…what the state variously means and does … for people in India today" (Fuller & Harriss 2000: 10). Above all, perspectives on the everyday activities of the state break down any easy distinctions between 'state' and 'citizens' or 'civil society'. As Osella and Osella comment, "the state is composed of people, and … analytical models which start from dualistic categories are bound to posit distance and overlook the quotidian intimacy of the state" (Osella & Osella 2000: 157), or fail to acknowledge networks of patronage, personalised relationships and shared cultural practices that link the state differentially to the people it is supposed to serve. Certainly, our own observations indicate that state employees do not abandon their personal social identities when they are at work. In other words, the distinction for individual government workers between their roles as public servants and as private individuals "concerned with their position in their own social world" (Fuller & Harriss 2000: 13) needs to be examined.

Some writers have explored the activities of the judiciary and the police as major instances of state-sponsored communalism. Certainly, too, some recent accounts of local riots have looked at the taken-for-granted underpinnings of discrimination against minority groups (Banerjee 1990; Brass 2002; Chakravarti et al. 1992; Das 1990; Engineer 1991a; Pandey 1991; Varadarajan 2002). Kohli is unusual for a political scientist in taking seriously the developmental activities of the Indian states, but he is primarily concerned with their regional, caste and class dimensions rather than community and gender (Kohli 1987). Little of this work deals in detail with gender issues. Further, communal disturbances by no means exhaust the local state's impact on people's daily lives. Rather, the local state encompasses all aspects of the interface between state and civil society.

Since 1991, the government of UP has been suffering from a fiscal crisis and organisations such as the International Monetary Fund (IMF) and the World Bank have prevailed upon it to reduce state spending as a means of trying to make the accounts balance. Funding allocations for the social sectors declined during the 1990s and actual implementation lagged even further behind allocations and the rhetoric of finance ministers (Mooij & Dev 2004). In 2000, moreover, the UP government negotiated a Good Governance and Fiscal Reform loan from the World Bank, and one of its conditions is that UP must make an annual 2 per cent cut in state employment. This, too, is likely to have a particularly adverse impact on the social sectors, since they have the largest workforces. Further, aside from 'rolling back the state', economic liberalisation in UP has facilitated a rapid expansion in the market for goods and services that have conventionally been seen as the responsibility of the state. In addition to the local state, then, we must also address the impact of economic liberalisation at the local level.

In the following account, we focus on the education and health care sectors, for several reasons. First, the lives of most women in rural Bijnor are framed by the everyday sexism that operates through domestic relationships. Women's links with the state and the market are largely mediated through their menfolk, who deal with agricultural extension workers or negotiate bank loans and so forth. The education and health sectors, however, have direct day-to-day relevance for girls and women, and issues of gender are writ large there. (We are most certainly not suggesting, however, that gender issues are irrelevant where women are apparently more marginal. Indeed, that very marginality in itself is a gender issue.) Second, education and health are crucial facets of the local state that (apparently) reflect the state's caring and paternalistic face and that are (in the developmental rhetoric) concerned with the disinterested provision of services on the basis of need. The state's capacity to control and differentiate among its citizens whilst performing its enabling and providing roles affords a particularly striking litmus test of the workings of the local state. We shall argue that the state education and health sectors are important sites where embedded systemic processes reflect and sustain – if not actively promote – structured inequalities. Further, the market's increasing inroads in these sectors during the 1990s have singularly failed to compensate for the growing inadequacies of state provision: supposedly market-neutral forces cannot deliver equitable provision in the face of pre-existing social and economic inequalities.

In brief, in the absence of energetic state action to counter existing inequalities and entrenched discriminatory patterns, education and health are important sites of gendered institutional communalism. Examining the position of Muslim women, in particular, in relation to education and health also enables us to return to the Hindu Right preoccupation with the 'backward' Muslim woman and with Muslim fertility.

Education in Rural Bijnor

If the data collected by the National Family Health Survey in 1998-99 are correct, most young people in rural UP are still functionally illiterate. Primary school enrolment rates in UP are lower than the all-India figures and the drop-out rates are higher than almost everywhere else in India (the main exception being Bihar). Many children attend school irregularly, and many do not successfully complete 5 years of schooling. Moreover, educational experiences are markedly skewed along gender lines: 10-14 year-old rural girls in UP have completed a median of 2.8 years of schooling, compared to 4.1 years for boys (Ramachandran 2003). Unfortunately, few data sets enable us to ascertain the profile of Muslim children's school enrolments. A recent exception, however, is based on the survey of 1993-94 carried out by the National Council for Applied Economic Research (NCAER) that indicates that Muslim children's school enrolments in India as a whole are significantly below those of caste Hindus, even when other factors are held constant (Borooah 2003: 80, 91). What lies behind these different patterns of enrolments and attendance? Here we shall first highlight three aspects of state primary schooling – location, quality and ambience – that have failed rural people in UP, especially girls and Muslims. Then we shall outline how non-state institutions have developed in response to these inadequacies, and consider some of the implications for Muslims and for rural girls.[4]

A crucial factor in UP has been the political influence of secondary teachers, which resulted in undue state expenditures on secondary sector facilities and, especially, on secondary teachers' salaries. Until about 1990, primary schooling had been the secondary sector's poor relation and the number of rural primary schools has consistently remained seriously out of kilter with the size of the cohorts of children of primary school age (see Gould 1972; Kingdon & Muzammil 2001; 2003; The Probe Team 1999). One consequence has been the intense competition over the location of new schools. Formally, district level government staff are responsible for sanctioning new educational facilities, but panchåyats (village councils) dominated by wealthy, well-connected landowners can often pull strings – whether at the district headquarters or in the state capital

– by donating land on which a school could be built (which helped to keep down the cost of expanding state education provision). Thus, for example, Qaziwala is by far the largest village in its vicinity, but the nearest government-aided secondary school is in Mandawali, 3 km away, because the wealthy Jat farmers there were able to establish a school and then ensure that it was financially assisted by the UP government. Moreover, dominant groups within villages succeeded in having schools located conveniently within their own controlled spaces. Such advantages may be cumulative. For example, government policy has increasingly drawn attention to the low enrolments of girls, and separate girls' primary schools have been established, but (for example, in Nangal) usually in the same villages, and often on adjacent plots. Such processes may not involve any conscious desire by officials to benefit one group rather than another. Nonetheless they tend to reinforce rather than to undermine existing inequalities.

Skewing of primary school locations is liable to be especially problematic for minority children and girls. If specific social groups dominate whole villages or some areas within villages, only the busier thoroughfares may be neutral ground. People from other castes or communities may feel uneasy and vulnerable to civilian policing of access if they stray alone into 'foreign territory'. Even quite young children will taunt or assault children from other castes or communities. Parents may be willing to send their children to schools only in neutral or friendly territory, or where they can create security in numbers. For girls, all public space is, in a sense, foreign territory. Unless protected by a brother or cousin, even girls from locally dominant castes are vulnerable to sexual harassment by boys from their own caste and community, let alone others, especially as they approach puberty. Few village girls continue beyond 5th class, aged 11 or 12, particularly if this involves travel beyond the village.

In UP generally, as in other parts of north India, the conditions of state primary schools are lamentable (Bashir 1994; Drèze & Saran 1995; The Probe Team 1999; Visaria et al. 1993; World Bank 1997). State primary schools in rural areas, in particular, have only rudimentary facilities, rarely more than a couple of classrooms, no matter how many students or classes. Learning resources are poorly understood and – as elsewhere in India – often locked away to avoid damage (Dyer 2000). The fabric of the buildings is likely to be in some degree of disrepair, and facilities such as drinking water or girls' toilets may be unavailable. Staffing is also a serious issue. Teacher absenteeism and lack of application whilst on the job are notorious in UP. Teachers have many other calls on their time, both official and personal: they often attend irregularly and actually teach for remarkably few days in the year. In addition, fear of sexual harassment makes rural postings problematic for women. Teachers from outside the immediate locality cannot be protected by their male relatives, whilst rural girls are still unlikely to obtain sufficient schooling to train as teachers.

The situation in Bijnor district reflects this general picture. The District magistrate provided us with a 2001 database giving details of primary (classes 1-5) and junior secondary (classes 6-8) school locations in the district, indicators of school quality, the numbers of teachers per school, enrolments, and the proportions of pupils by simple caste and religious indicators (General, i.e. Forward Castes; SC; OBC; and Minority, who are 94 per cent Muslim in Bijnor). Overall, despite the construction of some new buildings, class sizes are still large and the facilities poor. Moreover, those (relatively few) schools that are located where there are more Muslims (either as pupils or as neighbouring populations) are in more crowded facilities compared with schools in or near villages dominated by OBCs (mostly Jats) or other groups, or where there is no dominant group. Further, even if a school is accessible to its potential pupils, it may be difficult to ensure adequate staffing. Upper caste teachers, for instance, are likely to be less willing than Muslim and SC teachers to remain in postings in schools dominated by Muslims and SCs, and they work harder to be transferred away. These patterns are indicative of institutional discrimination: district officials are least responsive to Muslim and SC pressures to build schools in the first place, to repair them once they are built, to assign teaching posts to the schools, and to fill the posts when teachers are transferred away or retire. These schools also have the worst pupil-teacher ratios in the district and more teacher vacancies per school.

The ambience of schools is problematic for all rural children, for several reasons: the respect for the written word and emphasis on literary language and urban skills; the fixed timetable that sits uneasily with the demands of the agricultural cycle; the requirement to sit still for long periods; and the humiliation or physical punishments meted out to children who make mistakes or speak out of turn. If anything, however, the ambience of rural state primary schools tends to be least uncongenial for children from

Hindu backgrounds, whilst Muslim children's experiences of primary schooling are adversely affected by communal bias. Much of the debate during the late 1990s about the 'saffronisation' of education ignored the long-standing and insidious saffronisation of the state schooling system in small towns and villages in much of western UP, if not elsewhere.[5] In the early post-independence period, Urdu was downgraded to an optional language not available in all schools. Many Muslims saw this as an attempt by the state to undermine their allegiance to Islam and hamper their efforts to learn Arabic (Abdullah 2002; Ahmad 2002; Brass 1974; Farouqui 1994; King 1994; Latifi 1999; Lelyveld 1993; Pai 2002; Russell 1999a; 1999b; Venkatachaliah 1999). Textbooks dealing with citizenship, identity, the nation-state and Indian history (for instance, the impact of Muslim rule in India) have for long conveyed markedly pro-Hindu messages. Furthermore, the teaching establishment in UP has been dominated by Brahmans and other upper-caste Hindus (as well as OBCs such as Jats in Bijnor), a reflection of the role of the Hindi movement's activities during the earlier years of the 20th century (see Orsini 2002, and also Oesterheld 2006). An important feature of institutional discrimination is that it does not depend on overt bigotry and intentional bias. Many teachers, for instance, take for granted their own centrality in moulding India's citizens and they gravitate – often unthinkingly – towards culturally nationalistic models. In addition, though, the working practices of village school teachers are not effectively scrutinised and there is considerable leeway for overt discrimination to be part of normal school procedures. Even in the early 1980s, our Muslim informants in rural Bijnor were regularly alluding to the communalised ambience and functioning of state schools in the area. Many claimed that some teachers displayed distaste for things Islamic by, for example, refusing to make any allowances for Muslim students fasting during Ramzån. Others complained of teachers who gave Hindu pupils preference in marks and other privileges, or who favoured their own community when accepting pupils for tuition and favoured their tutees in class. The belief that such practices are endemic acted as a further disincentive for Muslim parents to take government schooling seriously. For Muslim parents, the presence of Muslim teachers would be an important indicator that their children would not be discriminated against, just as many parents prefer to send daughters to girls' schools, or to ones with female teachers.

For rural Muslim children, especially girls, the quality and ambience of the schooling environment have compounded the serious obstacles they faced in even accessing primary schools in the vicinity of their homes in the first place. In our four fieldwork villages in Bijnor, Muslims are still significantly under-represented in the state primary schools serving them – with only a handful of Muslim boys and sometimes even no Muslim girls at all.[6] Rural Muslims in Bijnor, then, were already facing problems in schooling their children well before the communal flashpoint in late 1990. And these problems of access, quality and ambience also predate the changes associated with 'economic liberalisation' and the fiscal crisis from which the UP state has been suffering since 1991.

With respect to primary schooling, since 1994 the World Bank has co-funded three successive projects in

UP (associated with the 'Education for All' programme) that have attempted to increase the school attendance of all children, especially girls. Bijnor became involved only in 2000. Local opinion is that these efforts remain largely 'on paper' and had made little difference by mid 2004. In secondary schooling, creeping privatisation was being experienced in the 1980s, largely by default. In Bijnor, from 1990, very few secondary schools were added to those receiving government aid, and very few new government secondary schools were established. Although the number of girls in secondary schooling grew, the numbers of boys attending these schools stagnated (except for boys from SC backgrounds, who benefited from special programmes). Even the locally dominant Jats, Brahmans and Rajputs were experiencing the limited accessibility and poor quality of state schooling. In response, newly prosperous landlords and rich peasant farmers, professionals and government servants (able to earn rental 'over-incomes') began to buy privilege for their children through private schooling, whether under caste or community control or commercially driven. These develop-ments accelerated towards the end of the 1990s.[7]

Most private schools in Bijnor District are established in towns, run by dominant Hindu caste groups mainly catering for their own children, and charge fees. Private primary schools established in the rural areas tend to be located on the verandas or in the courtyards of large village houses of the dominant Hindu castes. Their facilities are extremely limited. The teachers are often young educated men and women from similar backgrounds to the school managers. Few have formal teaching qualifications, but fear of losing their jobs tends to make for more regular attendance than in the state sector. On the other hand, levels of teachers' pay compare very unfavourably with those in the state sector, and the teachers (particularly the men) are a rather fluid labour force on the look out for better prospects elsewhere. The provision of private schooling in Bijnor is seriously skewed, then, and does little to rectify the problems of access, quality and ambience that confront Muslims in the state sector. Few local Muslim men or women are equipped to teach in them. In any case, many school managements have an overt ideological bias, such as affiliation to the RSS. And the fees and other costs associated with schooling (uniforms, books, etc) act as a further disincentive. Schooling is becoming more exclusive and expensive, and what are locally regarded as the 'best' schools are largely the preserve of urban, upper-caste Hindus, especially boys, from relatively wealthy households.

In brief, processes of privatisation are creating an increasingly differentiated schooling market. This is despite the absence of any clear or conscious policy (indeed, Ministers deny that privatisation is happening). Over the years, though, policy 'decisions' about education – about the location of schools, their funding, permitting the growth of the private sector, and so forth – have been taken according to the normal everyday functioning of the state at the local as well as the provincial level. The outcomes have been systematically biased against those sectors of society with the least leverage. 'Normal' decision-making leaves their interests out of account and structures the schooling their children receive. The state education sector has failed rural Muslims in Bijnor. So, too, has the market. Rural

Muslims tend to live in villages without state schools and their daughters' access to nearby state schools is curtailed because of the communal ambience of the school itself or because of harassment en route. Non-state schools are scarcely more accessible and they may be ruled out because of cost as well as ambience. Many rural Muslim children – especially girls – still receive no formal education at all. Evidence from other parts of India indicates that Muslim parents do send their children to schools – if they are accessible and affordable – and relatively wealthy urban Muslims in Bijnor district do the same.

Increasingly, though, rural Muslim children in the district are attending madrasahs. The marked growth in the madrasah sector since the 1980s is, to a considerable degree, a response to the lack of accessible schools and to the exclusionary and discriminatory practices of upper caste Hindu teachers, managers, administrators and management committees. Madrasahs charge nominal fees (at most) because they are funded by donations. The teachers are all Muslim. Madrasah pupils learn at least the basics of Islamic doctrine and morality; some madrasahs also teach Hindi and are recognised by the UP government up to 5th class or beyond. Muslim parents emphasise that madrasah education enhances their daughters' marriage prospects, and girls outnumber boys in the elementary classes in some rural madrasahs. Few girls continue attending a madrasah beyond puberty, however, because advanced schooling would not enhance (and might even damage) their marriage chances. Boys therefore predominate in the advanced classes. As would happen if they were in school, Muslim girls attending madrasahs are immersed in a regime that largely reflects rather than challenges conventional gender rela-tion-ships and that valorises their future lives as wives and mothers: the importance of modest, clean and docile bodies for fasting and reciting prayers or the Qur'ån Sharðf, and the moral tales (including selections from Bahishti Zewar) that emphasise the necessity of acquiring home-making skills and eulogise compliant domesticity (Metcalf 1990; Mukhopadhyay & Seymour 1994; Papanek 1979; Sharma 1986; P. Jeffery et al. 2004).

As we have indicated in Chapter 1, boys' education is locally regarded as a preparation for employment. In all castes and communities, parental strategies about girls' education are crucially linked to the (perceived) employment prospects of potential bridegrooms. Whilst young men increasingly want educated wives, they do not want ones who are more educated than themselves: thus girls' education tends to follow in the wake of that of their likely marriage partners. In Bijnor, as in most of north India, Brahmans and (increasingly) Jats and other landed Hindus have used their educational headstart to help their sons monopolise 'good' jobs (meaning secure, government or white collar). Muslims and SCs, (as well as to a lesser extent, the 'small' castes) cannot operate the levers of power in the same way. They believe their sons will not obtain 'good' jobs, because they lack the contacts (safårish) and the money to pay bribes (rishwat) that are needed over and above academic qualifications. Madrasah education offers Muslim boys little chance of successfully competing for secure white collar employment, other than as a maulvð or imåm, one of the few routes to non-manual and possibly urban employment for able rural Muslim boys.

Thus, rural Muslim parents tend to consider that schooling has little value for their sons' job prospects. In Bijnor, there are marked class differentials in school attendance among Hindus, but these are not paralleled amongst Muslims: Muslim, SC and 'small caste' Hindu boys drop out of schooling earlier than their upper caste Hindu counterparts in comparable economic positions.

Few rural Muslim girls remain in formal education, even in the madrasah, long enough for literacy to be firmly established. Most do not learn to read Hindi, which could enable them to negotiate shopping, transport and official business. Completion of primary schooling, of course, is a precondition for admission to middle and secondary schools, an outcome that is remote from the ambitions of most Muslim boys and girls alike in rural Bijnor. In any case, all the state and non-state junior high schools and higher secondary schools (classes 9-12) are located in towns and attendance (particularly of rural girls, irrespective of religious community) is also liable to be compromised by transport problems and costs.

In brief, then, the problems of school locations, quality and ambience mean that obtaining even primary schooling is highly problematic for rural Muslim girls. The low levels of Muslim girls' education, though, also need to be viewed in the wider context of the employment market for young Muslim men. The skewing of school attendance by community, gender, class and caste has implications beyond the higher levels of education to adult livelihood prospects. But these patterns of discrimination can be rectified only if gendered institutional communalism ceases to be endemic in the education sector and if Muslim parents believe that educating their sons would translate into enhanced employment prospects.

Health and Family Welfare in Rural Bijnor

Many of the processes we have described for schooling also affect the provision of health services. [8] Among Muslims and Hindus alike, gender differences in health status and access to health services are closely associated with the sexism of domestic life. Recent discussions of the routine workings of government health and family welfare facilities, indeed, have emphasised gender issues, along with class, but communal issues have rarely been addressed. Nevertheless, access to health and family welfare services in rural Bijnor is systematically skewed along all three dimensions. As with education, the public resources available to deal with health issues are severely limited, and poorly-regulated, often low-quality but usually expensive private providers are increasingly important. Combined with poor quality public facilities, in emergencies people have few alternatives to risking significant financial resources in attempts to get treatment for their families. Patterns of institutional sexism and communalism in health can thus be more disastrous than in the case of education.

The rural public health system in India was established after Independence, but to a considerable degree it followed patterns proposed in the Bhore report, submitted to the colonial Government in 1946 (Jeffery 1988). In establishing a hierarchy of sub-centres, Primary Health Centres (PHCs), sub-district and district hospitals and health facilities, the government relied in part on local resources: villages were expected to provide land for clinics, and sometimes the buildings as well. As with education, then, well-connect-ed and wealthier villages were able to attract government facilities to their territory. Locally dominant groups put pressure on district health officials, and offered plots of land to obtain clinics, despite poor locations or existing facilities nearby. Thus, the processes by which rural clinics are located in one place rather than another, or are allocated doctors, are not neutral, technical activities, any more than in the case of schools.[9] For example, in the 1960s, Man-dawar, in the physical centre of the Mohammadpur Deomal Community Development Block (which includes Dharm-nagri and Jhakri), with excellent road communications and a population of about 10,000 (70 per cent Muslim), was the obvious location for the PHC to serve the Block. But the PHC was sited at the far north border of the Block, and has never played a significant role in the lives of its residents. Similarly, Dharmnagri (with a Hindu population) is on no bus routes and yet has a clinic – whilst Qaziwala (with three times the population, but predominantly Muslim) has only a small sub-centre in a tumble-down rented building, and nearby Begawala (also mainly Muslim) is on a main road, has a well-attended weekly market and several small private pharmacies, and yet no government health facility. Nangal has a sub-centre in excellent premises located un-der the residence of the wealthy Jat landowner who was pradhån (village headman) when it was established, and there are more health facilities in several nearby larger, Hindu-dominated, villages.

The siting of health facilities has considerable influence on women's access to health care. Women's own work is time-consuming and they can easily use only those clinics a short walk from home. It is hard for a chaperon to take time to accompany them any great distance and women may not be permitted to go by themselves, or may find it too difficult to trail several small children along with them. Most people who attend government clinics come from within 5 km, and females (especially girls) are under-represented among clinic users (Arokiasamy & Pradhan 2004; Pandey et al. 1998; United Nations 1998). There are continuing attempts to ensure that child survival and safe motherhood programmes are developed in UP to reduce the appalling levels of infant mortality (76 per 1000 live births in 2003, 84 for girls and 69 for boys, according to Registrar General & Census Commissioner 2005) and maternal mortality (707 per 100,000 births in 1997, according to Department of Medical Health and Family Welfare 2000: 48). While the number of clinics and their accessibility to women remains so low and unevenly distributed, however, it is inevitable that many sub-groups will experience much higher mortality levels than these.

The services available at government health care facilities – what is provided in practice and the general ambience of that provision – are liable to be problematic for women in general. For instance, clinic staff may commute from town rather than live in the quarters that are often provided on the clinic compound. Rural postings provide less opportunity for private practice and staff may expend considerable effort in obtaining transfers to more attractive postings. Thus, clinic hours are not routinely observed and many staff report for duty irregularly.[10] Further, the residential quarters supposedly provided for female staff do not always exist, or are often seriously inadequate in terms of 'security' and comfort. Consequently, round-the-clock service by female staff (to deal with obstetric problems, for instance) is impossible – a serious limitation, since women patients prefer to consult female staff, particularly about gynaecological and obstetric matters. The lack of monitoring of staff also allows space for health workers to be highhandedly authoritarian or conspicuously disdainful about the capacity of village women in general to maintain proper hygiene at home.

Within this general picture of poor service, facilities for minority women are usually even worse. The staffing of medical facilities tends to reflect the greater access of dominant sectors of the population – men and upper caste Hindus, usually also from urban backgrounds – to education and training for medical and paramedical employment. According to Muslim women, many of these health employees are communal in their interactions with Muslims, as well as partial in their daily practices, for several reasons. One is the pressure on staff since the mid-1970s to achieve contraceptive targets. At some times in the year – in particular the winter, leading up to the end of the financial year at the end of March – much routine health work has been subordinated to government health workers' needs to 'motivate' women to 'accept' contraception, particularly sterilisation (see Chapter 1). Meeting family planning targets has been the main criterion on which health staff receive approval or punishment from superiors. Even since 1996, when the 'target-based approach' was abandoned in favour of a 'community needs assessment approach', contraceptive coverage remains a central feature of staff evaluations. Villagers told us of ANMs helping women through pregnancy and delivery only if they promised to be sterilised afterwards, or of persuading patients to accept interventions – especially contraception – without adequate monitoring for side-effects or consideration of the patient's best interests. Understandably, ANMs wanted postings where their sterilisation targets could be met relatively easily. Health workers generally found Muslims (as well as lower caste Hindus and the poor generally) hard to 'motivate'.

Government health policy (unlike education) requires staff to supplement clinic-based maternal and child health care by outreach activities that seek out pregnant women, infants and young children for immunisations and other preventive health services. In rural Bijnor, health workers (if anything) have tended to concentrate on cultivating relationships with members of relatively affluent, upper caste Hindu households (Jeffery & Jeffery 1996b; Jeffery & Jeffery 1997). Partly, this simply reflects their own social origins, although ingratiating themselves with influential village leaders can also enable them to influence where they are posted and protect female staff from harassment (Banerji 1973). But these are also the very households where they are more likely to 'motivate' family planning 'cases'. The upshot is that health workers rarely visit Muslim women in their homes – and if they make forays into Muslim villages or neighbourhoods, they may be suspected of doing so only in order to 'motivate' people for family planning.

Moreover, in our fieldwork villages, upper caste Hindu and Scheduled Caste women attended clinics to obtain tetanus toxoid protection during pregnancy and immunisations against whooping cough, measles, mumps, polio etc. for their children. The rates of immunisation of childbearing women and small children are substantially lower amongst Muslims.

Many of the government health service's inadequacies impinge on all women and the widespread local view – held by Hindus as well as Muslims – is that curative services are merely sweeteners to encourage people to accept contraception. But the prioritisation of family planning places Muslim women in an especially difficult position. Even 25 years after the Emergency, many rural Muslims regard health workers with suspicion and consider themselves specially targeted by the family planning programme. Muslim women complain about the local state's intrusive and coercive approach to family planning and its failure to meet women's perceived health care needs. In combination, the pro-natalism of some religious authorities, the absence of support for family limitation from husbands and mothers-in-law, and fears about how government health workers will respond to them make it difficult for rural Muslim women to obtain suitable modern contraceptives. They often prefer to consult private doctors who have no family planning targets to meet.

Many Muslims have also had unpleasant experiences of the 'pulse polio' programme, introduced in 1995 in response to pressure from donors to speed up the eradication of polio from India. Since 2000, at least four times a year government personnel – schoolteachers and village council officials as well as health personnel, and often with the support of organisations such as Rotary and Lions Clubs – come into villages and attempt to administer polio drops to all children under five years of age. 'Pulse polio' is one of the highest profile health-related government programmes. But continuing suspicion of government motives in relation to family planning has spilled over into the 'pulse polio' programme, and some rural Muslims, though by no means all, have resisted the programme because of a rumour that polio drops cause sterility. Increasing the coverage of polio immunisations has entailed some heavy-handed persuasion. Perhaps in part because of this focus on polio, immunisations for other childhood illnesses are at much lower levels. Other reasons are the inadequacies of the routine public health delivery system, and because such immunisations are not a normal part of private practitioners' repertoire.[11]

Developments in the 1990s, in any case, have further reduced people's faith in state services. As with education, health and family planning policy in India must also be seen in the wider context of economic liberalisation (for more on this see Qadeer et al. 2001; Rao 1999). In UP, there have been dramatic cuts in investment in clinic and hospital infrastructures (whether in the form of new buildings or the maintenance and upkeep of existing facilities), and steep declines in the recruitment of staff to expand provision or simply to replace staff who retire. In UP, per capita public expenditure on health in 1999-2000 was only about 85 per cent (in real terms) of that in 1990-91 (Mooij & Dev 2004: 102). The government dispensary in Dharmnagri was established in the 1950s and it has an impressive array of buildings – rarely used for the purposes for which they were built and even more dilapidated and down-at-heel now than in the 1980s. Like the government sector as a whole, there is little demand for its services, and staff spend much of their time chatting to one another in the compound. As in the early 1980s, villagers complain that government facilities rarely provide the drugs that are supposedly available. A recent World Bank report comments, 'In the poorer states such as Bihar and Uttar Pradesh, the public sector is completely dysfunctional and there are no effective alternatives to the private sector' (Radwan 2004: 13). According to National Sample Survey figures for India as a whole, over 80 per cent of out-patient care and nearly 60 per cent of inpatient care in 1995-96 was provided by the private sector (Radwan 2004: 10).

Certainly, the market in privately provided health care has expanded significantly in Bijnor's towns and also increasingly into its rural areas. In the early 1980s, for instance, just two private clinics in Bijnor town dealt with maternity cases, in addition to the government hospital. In 2004 there were at least a dozen, several of them run by (Hindu) women doctors. Villagers often depend heavily on the (illegal) private practices built up by government pharmacists, who are said to sell the free drugs intended for the poor (and persuade their superiors to turn a blind eye). In Bijnor's rural hinterland, the past decade or so has also seen the flourishing of numerous independent medical practitioners, all male but not necessarily trained in any of the medical traditions present in India (allopathic, homeopathic, ayurvedic or unånð). Generally, they run small enterprises from roadside stalls and kiosks, and they charge fees for their services and the medicines they recommend. They are mostly Hindu, but a few are Muslims. Private practitioners have also penetrated the home: around half of all deliveries in Dharmnagri and Jhakri in the late 1990s entailed the administration by untrained practitioners of injections to augment labour – a practice that, without adequate monitoring facilities, may seriously compromise the safety of the labouring woman and her child. Generally, villagers think that urban clinics provide more comprehensive and reliable services than rural practitioners, for instance, for cases requiring an operation or other in-patient care. But few clinics have been established by Muslims: in the health sector, there is nothing equivalent to the madrasah in education. Muslims in UP are disproportionately located towards the bottom of the class hierarchy, and few have the training or financial resources to establish a sizeable facility, least of all one providing free or heavily subsidised health care and medicines.

As with education, the markets in health care – both government and private – are heavily skewed. Government facilities are usually, but not always, cheaper than private medical care and most of their patients are people from the bottom of the economic heap. Yet government hospitals are also reckoned to have the best trained staff, and those with contacts and/or money may prefer to consult government doctors for complicated cases. On balance, most health benefits of government expenditures in UP go to the relatively well off: UP is either the worst or in the bottom three of the larger Indian states in any comparison of the poverty-related public expenditures on health (Mishra 2005: 76-77). Villagers sometimes comment that only 'important' people can get good care from public hospitals.

Private doctors (including government doctors working from their own homes or private clinics) provide advice and medication for widely differing fees – and the 'best' facilities are accessible only to the wealthiest households, for whom the increased availability of private medical services has widened the opportunities for tackling childhood ailments. Most people nowadays – even poor Muslims – seek private medical treatment and expect health care to entail outlays. Many poor people endure ailments without medical care at all or find themselves locked into costly medical encounters that result in serious debt. Private practitioners are mostly regarded in a positive light in comparison with government staff, who are generally said to deal with patients in a demeaning style, and to discriminate against Muslim and lower caste patients. But many villagers say that private practitioners are running a business (vyåpårð, the term used for market traders, dealers, merchants and the like) and are interested only in patients who can pay the medical charges to the full ('money itself discriminates', as one woman put it). Rudeness and overt discrimination would damage a practitioner's reputation and thus be bad for business. By the same token, practitioners' incomes are enhanced through running medical stores (pharmacies) and by medicalising self-correcting conditions or over-prescribing antibiotics and other drugs.

The state, then, is becoming less involved in people's health care, with immunisation programmes and family planning being the main exceptions to this. Government medical services are widely held in low esteem and rural Muslim women are by no means alone in regarding them as fine exemplars of the woeful faults that are thought to riddle government services in general. For Muslim women, though, the legitimacy of government health facilities is additionally undermined because of the government family planning programme. In 2000, the UP government announced that it wanted to achieve 'replacement level fertility' through a 'robust policy', by raising the use of contraceptives from about 28 per cent to 61 per cent by 2016 (Department of Medical Health and Family Welfare 2000: Preface, 18).[12]

Professionals in both education and health care sectors tend to devalue the education that takes place in the home, workshop or fields, or the contributions made to health status by nutrition or desī (country or traditional) medicines. Yet education and health care take place in many sites and are both much more than a matter of what is provided by dedicated institutions, whether state funded or private. Although people in rural Bijnor critique the local state and the market alike, however, government and private schooling and health care are valued – and scarce – resources. There is a demand for good education and for user-friendly family planning and health services, provided by the state and free or cheap for users. Systematic biases in the functioning of schools have long-term implications for children's life-chances (and thus for social stratification). Only formal schooling can provide the credentials that might widen access to formal sector employment (at least for some people). Similarly, cosmopolitan medicine plays an important role in curative health care, and people's ability to obtain it is systematically skewed in contemporary north India. Overall, Muslims in rural Bijnor have poorer access to government education and health services than comparable Hindus – and their disproportionate location towards the bottom on the economic heap prevents them from compensating for the institutionalised communalism of the local state system by buying these services in the marketplace.

The Hindu Right, Muslim Women and Engendered Communalism

The appalling drama of communal riots has rightly attracted attention. Our central argument here, though, is that we must also focus on times of apparent communal peace and the quotidian yet profoundly communalised processes that have systematically worked to the disadvantage of Muslim women.

Hindus in rural Bijnor often reiterate elements of the common wisdom about Muslims in India – that Muslims are 'backward' because few Muslim girls attend school and that they display their unpatriotic orientation through their wilful resistance to family planning and their purported determination to outnumber Hindus. In Chapter 1, we showed that the fertility of rural Muslims is somewhat higher than that of comparable Hindus, whilst this chapter indicated that school enrolments are indeed lower for Muslims (and especially for Muslim girls) than for other sectors of the rural population. Our discussions with rural Muslims, however, provide absolutely no support for the Hindu Right contention that Muslims are inherently hostile to education or that their fertility levels reflect an intentional strategy to outbreed Hindus. Muslim patronage of madrasahs and their fear of the government's family planning programme may contribute to the perpetuation of the common wisdom. But Muslims are not the only actors here. Systematic differences between Muslim women and other women do not result solely from processes internal to the community. The development and functioning of the education and health sectors reflect a very complex choreography, in which the involvement of the local state and of local elites is crucial.

Whether as employees of the state or as consumers of its services, local elites have ensured that scarce government facilities function to their advantage. Minority populations (and the poor in general) are weak constituencies in this competition. They face difficulties in putting pressure on the local state to provide accessible schools and health facilities. They are less able to benefit from the day-to-day discretion that local level state employees exercise in their work. Even with suitable education, Muslims generally lack the caste- and community-based contacts within the local state that can provide some men from the dominant Hindu castes with access to employment. For those – including Muslims in rural Bijnor – who believe that upper caste Hindus have a hold over desirable job opportunities for young men in the district, education seems an expensive and fruitless investment and there is little financial impetus for family limitation. Moreover, by responding to Muslim pressure to protect Islamic culture by officially recognising madrasah education, the local state (in effect) endorses the failure of madrasahs to provide Muslim children with the credentials (especially literacy in Hindi) necessary to become fully-fledged citizens. And poverty ensures that the increasingly salient markets in education and health care do nothing to redress the imbalances.

Upper caste Hindus are precisely those most prone to voice the common wisdom about Muslims and the most readily mobilised by organisations of the Hindu Right. Yet, ironically, it is their own domination of local social and political processes that has been crucial in generating and sustaining systematic communal and gender biases in the education and health sectors. All in all, these imbalances demonstrate the profoundly communalised and gendered character of local society and of the local state, and the significance of inequality, not simply of difference. Upper caste Hindus, then, are deeply implicated in the processes that disadvantage Muslim women – processes that have rather little to do with 'Islamic tradition'. The chains of causation and responsibility, in other words, are not as the Hindu Right likes to portray them.

At the beginning of this chapter, we highlighted some reasons why women in rural Bijnor are unlikely to mobilise around gender issues, despite their critiques of everyday sexism. Indeed, everyday sexism is itself a key reason why women in rural north India do not form a powerful political constituency to counter the continual endorsement and replication of the deep-seated gender inequalities that they experience in their everyday lives. Women are largely contained within households and have few resources that could oil the wheels of the political system. Thus they are poorly placed to exert much influence on the local state or to ensure that educational and health care facilities meet their priorities. Equally, the lack of woman-friendly health care and educational facilities in the rural areas itself has implications for women's mobilisation. Low fertility or improved health do not in themselves liberate women, but without access to good health care, women whose lives are devoted to childbearing, childrearing and domestic and farming work, have insufficient energy and time for political activism. Similarly, girls' schooling does not necessarily remedy women's domestic situations, provide economic independence and autonomy, or enable women to mobilise, although distance communication is undoubtedly more difficult for the non-literate (Jeffery & Basu 1999). Yet low levels of school attendance leave girls (especially in the rural areas) with little room for manoeuvre.

To these considerations, we must now add a further dimension. Muslim women are not simply disadvantaged as women. Rather, for them, everyday sexism in their domestic lives articulates perniciously with the everyday communalism that inflects normal village life, and with the processes of engendered communalism that are endemic in both the local state and in the market. Women from different communities – through their relationships to their male kin – are located in different ways in the wider society, including in relation to the local state and the market. Such processes heighten women's identification as members of religious communities and compromise their identification as women by driving a wedge between women of different communities. For instance, the prominence of madrasahs in rural Muslim children's education adds an additional twist to the communalisation of educational provision. As we noted above, Muslim girls' experiences of madrasah education (if any) tend to reinforce the sexism of family life and their economic dependency. Beyond that, madrasahs shield their pupils from direct exposure to the communalist ambience of schools. But this is at the expense of encapsulating Muslim girls within their own community – and educating children of different communities separately inhibits the growth of social links between them and gives space for the development of mutual ignorance (if not mutually hostile stereotyping) (Sikand 2001a; Sikand 2001b). Indeed (as we noted earlier), women are not immune to communal stereotyping and they are often directly involved in sustaining communal distinctions. In such circumstances, the mobilisation of women around issues of gender politics is extremely unlikely.

Nor are women's interests likely to be taken up by others. In western UP, there are few NGOs and even fewer women's groups that might facilitate women's mobilisation and empowerment (unlike in other parts of South Asia, perhaps most notably Bangladesh). Currently, too, despite the mouthing of commitments to girls' education and women's health, the programmes of local political parties take fundamental aspects of everyday sexism for granted, rather than challenging it. In any case, political parties are fighting over community, class and caste allegiances, and the remedying of gender inequalities is not an important political plank. Indeed, feminists' attempts to build allegiances among women have received a particularly hostile press from parties associated with politicised religion in India (and elsewhere in the region), on the grounds that feminism is an inauthentic and discreditable instance of cultural imperialism (Jeffery & Basu 1999). Moreover, the eclipsing or even erosion of religious community as a source of social identity would not necessarily result in the greater foregrounding of women's identities as women. Leftist organisations, for instance, have been notoriously slow to attend to women's concerns and to afford the space in which their identifications as women are tolerated. On the contrary, women's activism is all too often construed as a means by which the class becomes divided against itself and distracted from its opposition to its Other. Women in such organisations face continual struggles to keep concerns for gender equity on the agenda (Basu 1993; Omvedt 1993; Rose 1992; Sen 1990).

Of course, this is not to foreclose the possibility that NGO activism, political parties, or indeed government-sponsored interventions, might widen the opportunities for significant changes at some stage. But the present situation provides little scope for optimism. The processes that we have outlined here reflect everyday yet resilient patterns of local power politics, in which women cannot easily intervene. The trope of the backward Muslim woman and of Muslim high fertility seems likely to remain a critical and destructive barrier to improved health and education for them, as well as a severe constraint on better inter-communal relationships in north India.

Notes

[1] Since 1982 women's fashions have changed, and young Hindu women may wear a bodice instead of a kurta. Also, many houses, in Dharmnagri and Jhakri alike, now have 'latrines' with septic tanks.

[2] On Id-ul-Fitr many Muslim men go in procession to attend special prayers, often in the open, and then return home to break their fast. Tijo, or Teej, is marked by fasting, folk songs, and dancing as Hindu women recall Parbati's devotion to her husband Shiva. Married women visit their fathers' homes, where they receive gifts from their male kin, and an elaborate feast. Unmarried women who fast on this day are believed to have good luck in finding a suitable husband; married women who fast will find their husbands are faithful.

[3] Holi, originally a festival to celebrate good harvests and fertility of the land, is celebrated on the day after the full moon in early March. It is linked to stories from Hindu mythology involving fires and fun

with coloured powder and water, and is an excuse for Indians briefly to shed some of their inhibitions.

4   The passages in this chapter dealing with education have been substantially revised and are informed by the research in Bijnor that we conducted in 2000-2 with Craig Jeffrey. More details on the issues addressed here, in particular, the privatisation of secondary schools and Muslim children's education, can be found in our recent and forthcoming publications (P. Jeffery et al. 2004; 2005a; 2005b; Forthcoming; R. Jeffery et al. 2005c; 2006).

5   As Minister for Human Resource Development during the NDA coalition governments of 1998-2004, Dr Murli Manohar Joshi played a key role in the government's manifest attempts to legitimate a saffron version of Indian citizenship: for instance, changing the content and orientation of school textbooks and enhancing the roles of the 'Saraswati Shishu Mandirs' (primary schools) and 'Saraswati Vidya Mandirs' (secondary schools) run by the RSS.

6   On the other hand, in state primary schools across Bijnor District the barriers are no longer strong enough to prevent SC children registering, and probably attending, in considerable numbers. But the growth in their attendance has come at precisely the time when the quality of the schooling (measured by class sizes etc) has deteriorated most, and when private schooling has grown in significance.

7   Official policy to ensure access to state schools by SC children and by girls – e.g. using scholarships and fee waivers – somewhat mitigated the effects of these developments. But there were no special provisions for Muslims until after 2001. By the end of the 1990s, more children were attending secondary schools in Bijnor district than a decade earlier – but a far higher proportion was in private schools, where SC and Muslim children (especially Muslim girls) are severely underrepresented.

8   This section has been revised in the light of our research in 2002-4.

9   Unfortunately, we do not have as much data on location and quality of health care facilities related to population of the village and surrounding villages as we have for schools, but where we do have information it supports the same general conclusions.

10   According to spot-checks conducted in UP health centres in 2004, 46 per cent of doctors and 42 per cent of other staff were absent on days when they should have been present (Radwan 2004: 51).

[11]   Complete immunisation rates in India are still only around 35 per cent, a figure that falls to below 20 per cent for the poorest 40 per cent of the population. Rates in UP and Bihar are below even these figures (Radwan 2004: 5).

[12]   Donor involvement (particularly by USAID) in UP's health programmes is increasing: see http://www.usaid.gov/policy/budget/cbj2005/ane/pdf/386-014.pdf for details.

Afterword

The three essays in this volume were originally written between 1995 and 2003. Where possible we have updated them for this volume. But the relationship between religion and population growth has remained a highly contentious topic, academically and politically, and we have been unable to make all the changes we would have liked. In this Afterword, then, we address some of the points raised in the special issue of Economic and Political Weekly of 29 January 2005, and in a response made by Mari Bhat in March 2005.

The nine main articles in the January EPW issue present a range of tables of comparative statistics that allow readers to see Hindu and Muslim population totals in the different states and districts of India, and differences between Hindus and Muslims according to some basic indicators (rural-urban distribution, literacy etc.). A major contribution of the issue as a whole is that several of the articles provide something that we requested several years ago: analyses of the statistical relationships between membership of religious community and fertility that control for the effects of residence, region, schooling and social class.

The common conclusions of the papers can be summarised as follows. As far as mortality is concerned, they show that, controlling for region and residence, Muslim infant and child mortality rates are between 7 and 23 per cent below those of Hindus, depending on the survey and the indicator. Muslim adult mortality rates are also between 7 and 20 per cent below those of Hindus (Bhat & Zavier 2005: 389-90; Rajan 2005: 440). None of the papers spends much time trying to understand why this might be so, perhaps on the grounds that, substantial as these differences are, they make a relatively small contribution to differences in the population growth rates of Hindus and Muslims in India. But, as Bhat and Zavier note, these differences in mortality rates do pose an intellectual puzzle, given the evidence of the generally worse economic positions of Muslims (Bhat & Zavier 2005: 390). It is possible that some of the differences in infant and child mortality might be a result of greater 'daughter aversion' among Hindus, contributing to the more masculine sex ratios of living Hindu children (see Borooah & Iyer 2005). On the other hand, maternal mortality is usually higher for women who have more children, so we would expect Muslim maternal mortality rates to be higher than those of Hindus – but this has apparently not been explored in detail. Clearly, the whole topic of differences in child and adult mortality needs further investigation. By contrast, that is not the case for international migration or conversions from Hinduism to Islam: contra Saffron Demographers, the consensus is that neither of these factors is at all significant in understanding differential population growth rates (Bhat & Zavier 2005: 390).

Most of the papers focus on fertility. We shall not go into the finer details of the estimates of fertility, in part because of the range of possible indicators: some (such as the number of live births per 1000 women aged 15-45) are relatively simple; others (such as the Total Fertility Rate) are more complicated; yet others (such as estimates of contraceptive use, or statements about desired family size) have indirect relationships to the number of children actually born. But no matter which indicator of fertility is considered, nor which additional variables are used as controls, most professional demographers who have considered the question agree that the differences between the fertility levels of Hindu and Muslim women cannot be understood purely as a result of confounding factors such as where they live, how much schooling they have had, or how well off they are. Muslim fertility rates – even after allowing for the influence of these factors – are mostly above those of Hindus, except (according to some indicators) in Madhya Pradesh and Chhattisgarh (Bhat & Zavier 2005: 387; Rajan 2005: 444-5).

There is, however, considerable disagreement among these authors as to both the scale and the significance of the differences. Rather than going through each paper in turn we will make only a few important points here.

> Clearly, in India as a whole, Hindu and Muslim Total Fertility Rates (about 3.6 for Muslims in 1998-99 and about 2.8 for Hindus) are both well below what

is possible for populations where no form of contraception is being used.

Both populations tend to share considerable similarities with their neighbours from different religious commu-nities, often much more than they share with members of the same religious community who live in other parts of the country.

If we focus on the past 40 years or so, Muslim fertility started at a higher level than that of Hindus, but both populations are increasingly limiting their fertility, by one means or another.

The differences between the populations are declining in absolute terms: for example, Muslim women's use of contraception increased faster in the 1990s than that of Hindu women (Krishnaji & James 2005: 457). There is, then, good reason to think that Muslims birth-rates will fall steadily in the foreseeable future, and probably faster than Hindu rates will fall.

Because Muslim fertility started from a higher level, there is a 'demographic lag' effect: the total Muslim population is likely to continue to increase faster than that of Hindus because there are proportionately more young Muslim women; but (applying plausible assumptions) the share of Muslims in the population of the Republic of India is unlikely to exceed 20 per cent in the next 100 years (Bhat & Zavier 2005: 399).[1]

Even if these summaries of the current position are generally accepted by demographers, the question of explanation remains: why do these differences in fertility between Hindus and Muslims exist? In large measure our answer is given in Chapter 1 of this volume, based on our long engagement with trying to understand the daily lives of Hindus and Muslims, of different caste and class positions, in one district in western UP. Our account is founded on the argument that the slower decline in fertility amongst Muslims than amongst Hindus can – in Bijnor at least – be best understood through an understanding of the social situations in which Muslims find themselves, rather than as a result of 'Islamic theology' or Muslim political agendas.

Our approach has been criticised, in particular by Mari Bhat, on his own (Bhat 2005) and with Francis Zavier (Bhat & Zavier 2005). Bhat and Zavier are unhappy with our argument that it is important to look at different caste-like groups, at different regions, and at different social classes amongst the Hindus and the Muslims in attempting to understand their behaviour (Bhat & Zavier 2005: 385). They also reject our argument that 'discrimination in recruitment to public offices is the main source of the lack of interest of Muslims in acquiring higher education' (Bhat & Zavier 2005: 392). They deny our argument that communal propaganda has created a climate of fear and uncertainty about the future among Muslims, which would inhibit their willingness to reduce their fertility as quickly as Hindus in comparable situations (Bhat 2005: 1376; Bhat & Zavier 2005: 401). Bhat also claims that we underestimate the significance of 'religion' (compared to other variables such as education or urban residence). Finally, he finds it strange that we should have discovered that Jats were employing a variety of strategies (such as keeping some sons unmarried) to reduce fertility when we found no conscious strategies among Muslims to increase fertility (Bhat 2005: 1378).

Academics are used to detailed critiques of this kind, but they rarely interest a wider audience. Here we shall focus only on Bhat's general approach, which he usefully summarises. His main problems are with what he describes as the three variants of the 'minority hypothesis'.

1. Are Muslims denied basic government services, and does this exclusion result in their higher fertility?

2. Does Hindu nationalist propaganda evoke a defensive response that keeps Muslim fertility high?

3. Do communal riots and vilification campaigns make Muslims insecure and choose large families for self-protection?

Bhat rejects all three arguments, but provides unconvincing reasons for doing so. On the first argument, he says, 'several papers included in EPW's special issue have shown that the lower socio-economic position of Muslims can explain only a small portion of their higher fertility' (Bhat 2005: 1376). Therefore, he contends, it does not matter whether, or if so, why they are socially excluded, since this exclusion cannot explain higher Muslim fertility. Bhat's argument here is erroneous because he conflates 'low socio-economic position' and 'social exclusion', yet they are clearly not the same thing. If a group is poorer than another group, this may be the result of discrimination (though other possible explanations need to be considered as well). Social exclusion, however, includes how the members of the group perceive their condition, and how their perceptions of it affect their everyday lives. Lower fertility – stopping at two or three children rather than three or four – comes in part when people feel secure (in other words, when they feel 'included') and can realistically expect their first two or three children to survive and prosper economically. If 'socio-economic position' does not correlate closely with 'social exclusion' then the absence of a high correlation between socio-economic position and fertility is not very surprising, and certainly does not mean that there is no explanatory power in the argument that social exclusion helps to account for higher Muslim fertility. Put another way, the demographic evidence suggests that Muslims have higher fertility than Hindus in similar socio-economic positions, controlling for other variables. But, as we have shown in Chapter 3, Muslims are unable to make the same use of government and other facilities as comparable Hindus, they feel less secure about the future, and therefore tend to limit their fertility at higher levels than do Hindus.

Bhat's response to the second argument is also problematic. He argues that the propaganda of the Hindu Right would have more effect on Hindus – since they attend the public meetings or read the newspapers more than do Muslims. The net outcome would be to increase Hindu fertility, he says, rather than Muslim fertility. Bhat provides no evidence to support his position. His argument assumes that Muslims are not aware of what the Hindu Right says about them – yet we know from many studies how much news travels through informal means, through public readings of newspapers etc. As we can testify from our research in Bijnor, Muslims are only too aware of the Hindu Right propaganda – sometimes passed on by health personnel and teachers. This propaganda does tend to make Muslims fearful of the prospect of attack, to heed the call of 'Islam in danger', and to resist the messages of family planning programme staff. Here we suggest that Bhat's speculations ignore the relevant research.

The third argument – from feelings of insecurity – Bhat gives the praise of seeming 'plausible at first sight' (Bhat 2005: 1378). But, he says, any such reaction 'necessarily implies a conscious effort on the part of the minority group to increase its numbers' (Bhat 2005: 1378). We are not, however, talking about attempts to increase numbers: we are trying to explain a situation in which Muslim fertility declines later, or more slowly than that of Hindus. As we noted in Chapter 1, Dyson (1991) makes a strong case that early or rapid fertility decline is unusual, and it is this, rather than high or slowly declining fertility that needs to be explained. We find it useful to think in terms of a 'political economy of fatalism' (see, for comparable arguments, Popkin 1980; Scott 1985), or (taking the alternative of looking at people's hopes) of 'aspirations' (Appadurai 2004).[2] In highly stratified social systems, lack of cash, contacts and cultural capital all make it very hard for the poor and socially excluded to act with confidence. Where crucial resources are unequally distributed, what seems like 'fatalism' may be rather an accurate assessment of their poor chances of being able to take successful initiatives. People who are insecure – whether because they feel threatened with attacks or are routinely socially excluded – are less likely to have high aspirations for their children. Rather than accepting at face value people's statements that they have no choice (that they cannot use contraception because, for example, it is against their religion) it is important to look at the political, social and economic context within which such statements are made. Frequently enough, when the context changes, people are prepared to reject the views of their religious leaders. For example, Poland, Spain and Italy are three of Europe's most Catholic countries, and the Catholic Church has not changed its teachings against all forms of contraception – yet, with total fertility rates of 1.2 or 1.3, these three countries now have the lowest fertility in Europe (World Health Organisation 2005). We are certainly not suggesting that religious beliefs make no difference to fertility: in India it is true that Muslim women are much more likely than others to state that they are not willing to use contraception because they believe it to be against their religion. We intend to write about this in more detail elsewhere. Here we reiterate our argument that merely correlating material conditions or 'variables' without understanding the meanings that people attach to them and the contexts within which they arise is likely to result in misleading conclusions.

The wealthy and the socially included are more able to hold high aspirations. They are also more likely to invest in the high quality of a few children, because of the costs of educating, maintaining and settling them in secure marital and employment positions. In the specific case of our own research in Bijnor, we found some evidence of collective strategies among Jats to limit the number of legitimate sons and heirs. We found no comparable strategies amongst the Sheikhs to affect fertility one way or the other. There is nothing paradoxical here: Jats have a strong sense of security, based on their dominance of local politics, their networks and their wealth. Many can realistically expect to place their sons in good economic positions, either through land inheritance or through using influence to get them good jobs. This situation does not apply for the Sheikhs or other rural Muslims. In Bijnor (and, we hypothesise, in other parts of north India) most rural Muslims are excluded from this kind of social, political and economic security, and this helps to explain their slower response to social, political and economic pressures towards smaller families. Bhat claims that we do not produce evidence to support this argument: we can only assume that he does not count our kind of evidence as 'real', since our book Population, Gender and Politics (Jeffery & Jeffery 1997) lays out in considerable detail why we hold the views we do about the bases of fertility decision-making in Bijnor. Bhat counter-claims that the decline in the growth rate of Muslims is slower where communal riots are rare, or in decades when communal hostility was lower, and that this contradicts our argument. But this claim is not convincing. Correlating 'riots' with comparative rates of fertility decline in a simple manner assumes that riots have only an immediate and local effect, when their effects may be long-term and distant. For instance, our own recent research has confirmed that events distant in time (e.g. the attacks on Muslims after the mosque in Ayodhya was demolished in 1992) and distant in space (e.g. the 2002 attacks on Muslims in Gujarat) were very important aspects of Muslim understandings of their weak position in India. Assumptions about how people perceive threats to their own or their children's future need to be substantiated, rather than just asserted. Bhat should follow those demographers who analyse large-scale datasets to identify 'what needs to be explained' (Dharmalingam & Morgan 2004: 434; see also Dharmalingam et al. 2005: 529-30) rather than relying on speculation when the limits of such material are reached.

We do not wish to pursue these somewhat arcane academic discussions any further here, except to say that the recent debate does not change our view of why Hindu-Muslim fertility differences continue to exist. More importantly, perhaps, is whether the current political environment is likely to alter the context in which fertility decision-making takes place: as far as we are concerned, this means in particular the likelihood of public rhetoric and state provisions becoming more 'community neutral'. Unfortunately, the electoral defeat of the BJP in the 2004 national elections does not promise dramatic changes. The BJP's loss of power did not reflect a major swing away from right-wing parties, but rather the effects of opposition alliances and voting against incumbent MPs. Right-wing Hindus are still well-entrenched within the mass media, the judiciary and the education sector. So we doubt that the 'common wisdom' will be radically challenged. Admittedly, the Congress-led coalition has taken several steps to reduce the official support for these views (e.g. to remove the worst anti-Muslim stereotypes from the history textbooks), and we applaud these moves. But it has taken other steps that seem retrograde: with the support of external actors (whether the IMF, the World Bank, USAID or commercial interests), it remains strongly committed to the 'reform' agenda, through which the role of the state in public services in health and education across the country is reduced wherever possible.

Moreover, we cannot be sure that gender issues will be taken more seriously by the new government: national level proclamations of equal opportunities for women, minorities, and (especially) women from the minorities, show no serious engagement with the kinds of issues we have raised here. During the summer of 2004, for instance, the Common Minimum Programme of the newly elected central government issued new directives for a 'sharply targeted population control programme' in 150 high fertility districts. This will undoubtedly put pressure on health staff to meet family planning targets, at the expense of their maternal and child health activities – and reinforce the mistrust with which rural Muslims (and the poor generally) in north India regard the government health services. In the current context of global and Indian Islamophobia, however, without a concerted effort to deal with inequalities of all kinds, to pursue an energetic policy in favour of women's rights, and to protect the rights of minorities of all religious flavours, the patterns of social exclusion and social insecurity we have described in these pages will persist unchallenged.

Notes

[1] As we argued in Chapter 1 of this volume, however, these exercises are merely statistical and the predicted outcomes may or may not come to pass. We quote Bhat and Zavier's conclusion only to show that Saffron Demographers' methods and predictions are a very long way from those of professional demographers.

[2] We develop this argument further in Jeffery & Jeffery (2005).

Bibliography

Abdullah, H. 2002. Minorities, Education and Language: The Case of Urdu. *Economic and Political Weekly* 37, 24: 2288-2292.

Agarwal, B. 1994. *A Field of One's Own: Gender and Land Rights in South Asia*. Cambridge: Cambridge University Press.

—. 1997. "Bargaining" and Gender Relations: Within and Beyond the Household. *Feminist Economics* 3, 1: 1-51.

Agnes, F. 1992. Maintenance for Women: Rhetoric of Equality. *Economic and Political Weekly* 27, 41: 2233-2235.

—. 1995. Women's movement Within a Secular Framework: Redefining the Agenda. Pp.136-57 in *Women and the Hindu Right* (eds) T. Sarkar & U. Butalia. London & New Delhi: Zed Press & Kali for Women.

—. 1996. Economic Rights of Women in Islamic Law. *Economic and Political Weekly* 31, 41-42: 2832-2838.

—. 1999. *Law and Gender Inequality: The Politics of Women's Rights in India*. New Delhi: Oxford University Press.

Agnihotri, I. & V. Mazumdar. 1995. Changing Terms of Political Discourse: Women's Movement in India, 1970s-1990s. *Economic and Political Weekly* 30, 29: 1869-1878.

Agnihotri, S.B. 2000. *Sex Ratio Patterns in the Indian Population: A Fresh Exploration*. New Delhi: Sage.

Ahmad, A. 1967. *Islamic Modernism in India and Pakistan 1857-1964*. London: Oxford University Press (For Royal Institute of International Affairs).

Ahmad, I. (ed.) 1973. Caste and Social Stratification among the Muslims. Delhi: Manohar.

— (ed.) 1976. *Family, Kinship and Marriage among Muslims in India*. Delhi: Manohar.

— (ed.) 1981. *Ritual and Religion among Muslims in India*. Delhi: Manohar.

—. 2002. Urdu and Madrasa Education. *Economic and Political Weekly* 37, 24: 2285-2287.

— (ed.). 2003. *Divorce and remarriage among Muslims in India*. New Delhi: Manohar.

Ahmed-Ghosh, H. 1994. Preserving Identity: A Case Study of Palitpur. Pp.169-187 in *Forging Identities: Gender, Communities and the State* (ed.) Z. Hasan. New Delhi: Kali for Women.

Ali, M.M.H. 1832. *Observations on the Mussulmauns of India: Descriptive of their Manners, Customs, Habits and Religious Opinions (two volumes)*. London: Parbury, Allen and Co. (Reprinted in 1973 by Idarah-i Adabiyat-i Delli, Delhi).

Ahmed, L. 1982. Western Ethnocentrism and Perceptions of the Harem. *Feminist Studies* 8, 4: 521-34.

Anthias, F. & N. Yuval-Davis. 1992. *Racialised Boundaries: Race, nation, gender, colour and class and the anti-racist struggle*. London and New York: Routledge.

Anveshi Law Committee. 1997. Is Gender Justice Only a Legal Issue? Political Stakes in UCC Debate. *Economic and Political Weekly* 32, 9 & 10: 453-458.

Appadurai, A. 1993. Number in the Colonial Imagination. Pp.314-339 in *Orientalism and The Postcolonial Predicament: Perspectives On South Asia* (Eds) C.A. Breckenridge & P. van der Veer. Philadelphia: University of Pennsylvania Press.

—. 2004. The Capacity to Aspire. Pp.59-84 in *Culture and Public Action* (eds) V. Rao & M. Walton. Stanford, CA: Stanford University Press.

Arokiasamy, P. & J. Pradhan. 2004. Gender bias against female children in India: Regional differences and their implications for MDGs. http://www.nsu.newschool.edu/internationalaffairs/papers/arokiasamy.pdf. Last accessed on 29 July 2005

Bacchetta, P. 1993. All our Goddesses are Armed: Religion, Resistance, and Revenge in the Life of a Militant Hindu Nationalist Woman. *Bulletin of Concerned Asian Scholars* 25, 4: 38-51.

—. 1994. Communal Property/Sexual Property: On Representations of Muslim Women in A Hindu Nationalist Discourse. Pp.188-225 in *Forging Identities: Gender, Communities and The State* (Ed.) Z. Hasan. New Delhi: Kali For Women.

—. 1996. Hindu Nationalist Women as Ideologues: The Sangh, The Samiti and Differential Concepts of The Hindu Nation. Pp.126-67 in *Embodied Violence* (Eds) K. Jayawardana & M. De Alwis. New Delhi: Kali For Women.

Banerjee, A. 1990. Comparative Curfew: changing dimensions of communal politics in India. Pp.37-68 in *Mirrors of Violence: communities, riots and survivors in South Asia* (ed.) V. Das. Delhi: Oxford University Press.

Banerjee, N. 1998. Whatever Happened to the Dreams of Modernity? The Nehruvian Era and Women's Position. *Economic and Political Weekly* 33, 17: WS-2 - WS-7.

Banerjee, S. 1989. Marginalization of women's popular culture in nineteenth century Bengal. Pp.127-179 in *Recasting Women: Essays in colonial history* (eds) K. Sangari & S. Vaid. New Delhi: Kali for Women.

Banerji, D. 1973. Health Behaviour of Rural Populations: Impact of Rural Health Services. *Economic and Political Weekly* 8, 51: 2261-68.

Bardhan, P.K. 1974. On Life and Death Questions. *Economic and Political Weekly* 9, 1293-1304.

—. 1984. *The political economy of development in India.* Oxford: Blackwell.

Barth, F. (ed.) 1969. *Ethnic Groups and Boundaries.* Bergen: Univertsitetsforlaget.

Bashir, S. 1994. Public Versus Private in Primary Education: Comparisons of School Effectiveness and Costs in Tamil Nadu. Ph.D.: London School of Economics.

Basu, A. (Ed.) 1993. *Women and Religious Nationalism in India (Bulletin of Concerned Asian Scholars, Vol. 25 No. 4).*

—. 1995a. Feminism Inverted: the Real Women and Gendered Imagery of Hindu Nationalism. Pp.158-80 in *Women and the Hindu Right* (eds) T. Sarkar & U. Butalia. New Delhi: Kali for Women.

—. 1995b. Introduction. Pp.1-21 in *The Challenge of Local Feminisms: Women's Movements in Global Perspective* (ed.) A. Basu. Boulder: Westview Press.

—. 1995c. Why Local Riots Are Not Simply Local: Collective Violence and the State in Bijnor, India 1988-93. *Theory and Society* 24, 1: 35-78.

—. 1999. Hindu Women's Activism in India and the Questions it Raises. Pp.167-184 in *Resisting the Sacred and the Secular: Women and Politicised Religion in South Asia* (Eds) P. Jeffery & A. Basu. New Delhi: Kali for Women.

Basu, A. & A. Kohli (Eds) 1998. *Community Conflicts and the State in India*. Delhi: Oxford University Press.

Basu, A.M. 1996. The Demographics of Hindu Fundamentalism. Pp.129-156 in *Unravelling the Nation: Sectarian Conflict and India's Secular Identity* (Eds) K. Basu & S. Subrahmanyam. New Delhi: Penguin.

—. 1997. The 'Politicization' of Fertility to Achieve Non-Demographic Objectives. *Population Studies* 51, 5-18.

Basu, T., P. Datta, S. Sarkar, T. Sarkar & S. Sen. 1993. *Khaki Shorts, Saffron Flags*. Delhi: Orient Longman.

Beteille, A. 1992. *The Backward Classes in Contemporary India*. New Delhi: Oxford University Press.

Bhabha, H. 1990. *Nation and Narration*. London: Routledge.

Bhat, P.N. 1996. Contours of Fertility Decline in India: A District Level Study Based on the 1991 Census. In *Population Policy and Reproductive Health* (Ed.) K.N. Srinivasan. Delhi: Hindustan.

—. 2005. Trivialising Religion: Causes of Higher Muslim Fertility. *Economic and Political Weekly* 40, 13: 1376-79.

Bhat, P.N. & F. Zavier. 1999. Findings of National Family Health Survey: Regional Analysis. *Economic and Political Weekly* 34, 3008-3032.

Bhattacharya, S. 2003. Advani Backs 'Study' Saying Majority will be Minority Soon. *The Indian Express* 23 September.

Blunt, E.A.H. 1969. *The Caste System of Northern India*. Delhi: S. Chand.

Billig, M. 1995. *Banal Nationalism*. London: Sage.

Borooah, V.K. 2003. Births, Infants and Children: An Econometric Portrait of Women and Children in India. *Development and Change* 34, 1: 67-103.

Borooah, V.K. & S. Iyer. 2005. Religion, Literacy and the Female to Male Ratio. *Economic and Political Weekly* 40, 5: 419-27.

Bose, A. 2003. Population Research: Deteriorating Scholarship. *Economic and Political Weekly* 28, 44: 4637-39.

—. 2005. Beyond Hindu-Muslim Growth Rates: Understanding Socio-Economic Reality. *Economic and Political Weekly* 40, 5: 370-74.

Brass, P.R. 1974. *Language, Religion and Politics in North India.* London: Cambridge University Press.

—. 2002. *The Production of Hindu-Muslim Violence in Contemporary India.* New Delhi: Oxford University Press.

Butalia, U. 1997-8. Communalism: A New Challenge to the Women's Movement in India. *Journal of Women's Studies* 1, 2: 15-27.

Caldwell, J. 1986. Routes to Low Mortality in Poor Countries. *Population and Development Review* 12, 2: 171-200.

Caldwell, J.C., Barkat-E-Khuda, B. Caldwell, I. Pieris & P. Caldwell. 1999. The Bangladesh Fertility Decline: An Interpretation. *Population and Development Review* 25, 1: 67-85.

Cassen, R.H. 1978. *India: Population, Economy, Society.* London: Macmillan.

Chakravarti, U., P. Choudhury, P. Dutta, Z. Hasan, K. Sangari & T. Sarkar. 1992. Khurja Riots, 1990-91: Understanding the Conjuncture. *Economic and Political Weekly* 27, 18: 951-65.

Chamadia, A. & S. Gatade. 2003. Poison Myths: there's no correlation between religion and population growth. *The Indian Express* 5 November.

Chamie, J. 1977. Religious Differentials in Fertility: Lebanon, 1971. *Population Studies* 32, 2: 365-82.

Chant, S. 1997. *Women-Headed Households: Diversity and Dynamics in the Developing World.* Basingstoke: Macmillan.

Chatterjee, P. 2003. Demographic Demonology. *The Telegraph* 10 July.

Chaudhuri, M. 1996. Citizens, workers and emblems of culture: An analysis of the First Plan document on women. Pp.211-235 in *Social Reform, Sexuality and the State* (ed.) P. Uberoi. New Delhi: Sage.

Chen, M.A. (ed.) 1998. *Widows in India: Social Neglect and Public Action*. New Delhi: Sage.

Chen, M.A. & J. Drèze. 1992. Widows and Health in Rural North India. *Economic and Political Weekly* 27, 43-44: WS-81 - WS-92.

—. 1995a. Recent Research on Widows in India: Workshop and Conference Report. *Economic and Political Weekly* 30, 39: 2435-2450.

—. 1995b. Widowhood and Well-being in Rural North India. Pp.245-288 in *Women's Health in India: Risk and Vulnerability* (eds) M. Das Gupta, L.C. Chen & T.N. Krishnan. Bombay: Oxford University Press.

Chhachhi, A. 1989. The State, Religious Fundamentalism and Women: Trends in South Asia. *Economic and Political Weekly* 24, 11: 567-78.

—. 1991. Forced Identities: the State, Communalism, Fundamentalism and Women in India. Pp.144-75 in *Women, Islam and the State* (ed.) D. Kandiyoti. London: Macmillan.

—. 1994. Identity Politics, Secularism and Women: A South Asian Perspective. Pp.74-95 in *Forging Identities: Gender, Communities and the State* (ed.) Z. Hasan. New Delhi: Kali for Women.

Chhachhi, A., F. Khan, G. Navlakha, K. Sangari, N. Malik, R. Menon, T. Sarkar, U. Chakravarti, U. Butalia & Z. Hasan. 1998. UCC and Women's Movement. *Economic and Political Weekly* 33, 9: 487-488.

Chipp-Kraushaar, S. 1981. The All Pakistan Women's Association and the 1961 Muslim Family Laws Ordinance. Pp.263-285 in *The Extended Family: Women and Political Participation in India and Pakistan* (ed.) G. Minault. Delhi: Chanakya Publications.

Chowdhry, P. 1994. *The Veiled Women: Shifting Gender Equations in Rural Haryana 1880-1990*. Delhi: Oxford University Press.

Cohn, B.S. 1987. The Census, Social Structure and Objectification in South Asia. Pp.224-254 in *An Anthropologist Among The Historians and Other Essays* (Ed.) B.S. Cohn. Delhi & London: Oxford University Press.

Crooke, W. (ed.) 1921. *Islam in India or the Qanun-i-Islam*. Oxford: Oxford University Press (Reprinted in 1975 by Curzon Press, London).

Das, V. 1990. Introduction: communities, riots and survivors. Pp.1-36 in *Mirrors of Violence: communities, riots and survivors in South Asia* (ed.) V. Das. Delhi: Oxford University Press.

Datta, P. 1993. Dying Hindus: Production of Hindu Communal Common Sense in Early 20th Century Bengal. *Economic and Political Weekly* 28, 25: 1305-19.

—. 1999. *Carving Blocs--Communal Ideology in Early Twentieth-Century Bengal*. Delhi: Oxford University Press.

Davis, K. 1951. *The Population of India and Pakistan*. Princeton: Princeton University Press.

Dayal, J. 2003. Lies, Half Truths and Statistics: The fine art of demonisation as political demography. www.aiccindia.org/art26.htm. Last accessed on 12 December 2003 2003

Department of Medical Health and Family Welfare. 2000. *Proceedings of the Workshop on Population Policy for Uttar Pradesh*. Lucknow: Government of Uttar Pradesh.

Dharmalingam, A. & S.P. Morgan. 2004. Pervasive Muslim-Hindu Fertility Differences in India. *Demography* 41, 3: 529-45.

Dharmalingam, A., K. Navaneetham & S.P. Morgan. 2005. Muslim-Hindu Fertility Differences: Evidence from National Family Health Survey II. *Economic and Political Weekly* 40, 5: 429-36.

Drèze, J. & M. Murthi. 1999. *Fertility, Education and Development: Further Evidence from India.* STICERD, London School of Economics Development Economics Research Programme Working Paper 80.

Drèze, J. & M. Saran. 1995. Primary Education and Economic Development in China and India: overview and Two case Studies. *Choice, Welfare and Development* (eds) K. Basu, P. Pattanaik & K. Suzumura. Oxford: Clarendon.

Dyer, C. 2000. *Operation Blackboard: Policy Implementation in Indian Elementary Education.* Oxford: Symposium Books.

Dyson, T. 1991. Child Labour and Fertility: An Overview, an Assessment and an Alternative Framework. Pp.81-100 in *Child Labour in the Indian Sub-Continent: Dimensions and Applications* (Ed.) R. Kanbargi. New Delhi: Sage.

Dyson, T. & M. Moore. 1983. On Kinship Structure, Female Autonomy and Demographic Behavior in India. *Population and Development Review* 9, 1: 35-60.

Engineer, A.A. (ed.) 1984. *Communal riots in post-independence India.* Hyderabad: Sangam Books India.

— (ed.) 1987. *The Shah Bano Controversy.* Bombay: Orient Longman.

—. 1991a. The Bloody Trail: Ramjanmabhoomi and Communal Violence in UP. *Economic and Political Weekly* 26, 4: 155-59.

— . 1991b. *Mandal Commission Controversy.* Delhi: Ajanta Publications.

—. 1992. *The Rights of Women in Islam*. Delhi: Sterling Publishers.

—. 1999. Muslim Women and Maintenance. *Economic and Political Weekly* 34, 24: 1488-1489.

Fargues, P. 1993. Demography and Politics in the Arab World. *Population: An English Selection* 5, 1: 1-20.

Farouqui, A. 1994. Urdu Education in India: Four Representative States. *Economic and Political Weekly* 29, 14: 782-785.

Flyvbjerg, B. 2001. *Making Social Science Matter: Why Social Inquiry Fails and How It Can Succeed Again* (trans.) S. Sampson. Cambridge: Cambridge University Press.

—. 2004. Five Misunderstandings About Case-Study Research. Pp.420-434 in *Qualitative Research Practice* (eds) C. Seale, G. Gobo, J.F. Gubrium & D. Silverman. London and Thousand Oaks, CA: Sage.

Fuller, C. & J. Harriss. 2000. For an anthropology of the modern Indian state. Pp.1-30 in *The Everyday State and Society in Modern India* (eds) C. Fuller & V. Bénéï. New Delhi: Social Science Press.

Gangoli, G. & G. Solanki. 1997. Towards Gender Just Laws. *Economic and Political Weekly* 32, 16: 854-855.

Gardner, K. 1999. Women and Islamic Revivalism in a Bangladeshi Community. Pp.203-220 in *Resisting the Sacred and the Secular: Women's Activism and Politicized Religion in South Asia* (eds) P. Jeffery & A. Basu. New Delhi: Kali for Women.

Goldscheider, C. & P.N. Uhlenberg. 1969. Minority Group Status and Fertility. *American Journal of Sociology* 74, 4: 361-72.

Gopal, S. (Ed.) 1991. *Anatomy of A Confrontation: The Babri Masjid-Ramjanambhoomi Issue*. Delhi: Orient Longman.

Gould, H. 1972. Educational Structures and Political Processes in Faizabad District, Uttar Pradesh. Pp.94-120 in *Education and Politics in India: Studies in Organization, Society and Policy* (eds) S.H. Rudolph & L.I. Rudolph. Cambridge MA: Harvard University Press.

Greenhalgh, S. 1995. Anthropology Theorises Reproduction. Pp.3-28 in *Situating Fertility: Anthropology and Demographic Enquiry* (Ed.) S. Greenhalgh. Cambridge: Cambridge University Press.

Gupta, A. 1993. Blurred Boundaries: The Discourse of Corruption, the Culture of Politics, and the Imagined State. *American Ethnologist* 22, 2: 375-402.

Gupta, C. 1998. Articulating Hindu Masculinity and Femininity: 'Shuddhi' and 'Sangathan' Movements in United Provinces in the 1920s. *Economic and Political Weekly* 33, 13: 727-735.

—. 2002. *Sexuality, Obscenity, Community: Women, Muslims, and the Hindu Public in Colonial India*. New Delhi: Permanent Black.

Gupta, C. & M. Sharma. 1996. Communal Constructions: Media Reality Vs Real Reality. *Race and Class* 38, 1: 1-20.

Hall, S. 1991. Old and New Identities, Old and New Ethnicities. Pp.41-68 in *Culture, Globalization and the World-System: Contemporary Conditions for the Representation of Identity* (ed.) A.D. King. Basingstoke: Macmillan.

Hall, S., D. Held & T. McGrew (eds) 1992. *Modernity and its Futures*. Cambridge: Polity Press, in association with the Open University.

Hasan, M. 1988. Indian Muslims since Independence: in search of integration and identity. *Third World Quarterly* 10, 2: 818-42.

—. 1991. *Nationalism and Communal Politics in India*. Delhi: Manohar.

—. 1997. *Legacy of a Divided Nation: India's Muslims Since Independence*. Delhi: Oxford University Press.

Hasan, Z. 1989. Minority Identity, Muslim Women Bill Campaign and the Political Process. *Economic and Political Weekly* 24, 1: 44-50.

—. 1993. Communalism, State Policy and the Question of Women's Rights in Contemporary India. *Bulletin of Concerned Asian Scholars* 25, 4: 5-15.

— (ed.) 1994. *Forging Identities: Gender, Communities and the State*. New Delhi: Kali for Women.

—. 1999. Gender Politics, Legal Reform, and the Muslim Community in India. Pp.71-88 in *Resisting the Sacred and the Secular: Women and Politicized Religion in South Asia* (eds) P. Jeffery & A. Basu. New Delhi: Kali for Women.

Hendre, S. 1971. *Hindus and Family Planning*. Bombay: Supraja Prakashan.

Hodges, S. 2004. Governmentality, Population and Reproductive Family in Modern India. *Economic and Political Weekly* 39, 11: 1157-63.

Husain, S.A. 1976. *Marriage Customs among Muslims in India: A Sociological Study of Shia Marriage Customs*. Delhi: Sterling Publishers.

International Institute for Population Studies. 1995. *National Family Health Survey (MCH and Family Planning) - Uttar Pradesh, 1992-93*. Bombay: International Institute for Population Studies.

Jacobson, D. 1976. The Veil of Virtue: *Purdah* and the Muslim Family in the Bhopal Region of Central India. Pp.169-215 in *Family, Kinship and Marriage among Muslims in India* (ed.) I. Ahmad. Delhi: Manohar.

—. 1995. Women and Jewelry in Rural India. Pp.171-223 in *Women in India: Two Perspectives* (eds) D. Jacobson & S.S. Wadley. Delhi: Manohar.

Jacobson, D. & S.S. Wadley. 1995. *Women in India: Two Perspectives*. Delhi: Manohar.

Jaffrelot, C. 1996a. *The Hindu Nationalist Movement and Indian Politics 1925 To The 1990s*. London: Hurst.

—. 1996b. The Idea of The Hindu Race in The Writings of Hindu Nationalist Ideologues in The 1920s and 1930s: A Concept Between Two Cultures. Pp.327-354 in *The Concept of Race in South Asia* (Ed.) P. Robb. Delhi: Oxford University Press.

Jalal, A. 1991. The convenience of subservience: women and the state in Pakistan. Pp.77-114 in *Women, Islam and the State* (ed.) D. Kandiyoti. London: Macmillan.

Jayaraj, D. & S. Subramanian. 2004. Abusing Demography. *Economic and Political Weekly* 39, 12: 1227-36.

Jeffery, P.M. 1999. Agency, Activism, and Agendas. Pp.221-243 in *Resisting the Sacred and the Secular: Women and Politicized Religion in South Asia* (eds) P. Jeffery & A. Basu. New Delhi: Kali for Women.

—. 2000. Identifying Differences: Gender Politics and Community in Rural Bijnor, UP. Pp.286-309 in *Gender Constructs in Indian Religion and Society* (eds) J. Leslie & M. McGee. Delhi: Oxford University Press.

—. 2001. A Uniform Customary Code? Marital Breakdown and Women's Economic Entitlements in Western UP. *Contributions to Indian Sociology* 35, 1: 1-33.

Jeffery, P.M. & A. Basu (eds) 1999. *Resisting the Sacred and the Secular: Women's Activism and Politicized Religion in South Asia*. New Delhi: Kali for Women (also published in 1998 as "Appropriating Gender" by Routledge).

Jeffery, P. M. & R. Jeffery. 1994a. Killing My Heart's Desire: Education and Female Autonomy in Rural North India. Pp.125-171 in *Woman As Subject: South Asian Histories* (Ed.) N. Kumar. Calcutta & Charlottesville: Bhatkal and Sen & Virginia University Press.

—. 1996a. *Don't Marry Me to a Plowman: Women's Everyday Lives in Rural North India*. Boulder & New Delhi: Westview Press & Vistaar.

—. 1996b. What's The Benefit of Being Educated? Girls' Schooling, Women's Autonomy and Fertility Outcomes in Bijnor. Pp.150-183 in *Girls' Schooling, Women's Autonomy and Fertility Change in South Asia* (Eds) R. Jeffery & A. Basu. New Delhi: Sage.

—. 1998. Silver Bullet or Passing Fancy? Girls' Schooling and Population Policy. Pp.239-258 in *Feminist Visions of Development: Gender Analysis and Policy* (Eds) C. Jackson & R. Pearson. London and New York: Routledge.

Jeffery, P.M., R. Jeffery & C. Jeffrey. 2004. Islamisation, Gentrification and Domestication: An 'Islamic Course for Girls' and rural Muslims in Bijnor, Uttar Pradesh. *Modern Asian Studies* 34, 1: 1-53.

—. 2005a. The Mother's Lap and the Civilising Mission: Madrasah Education and rural Muslim girls in western Uttar Pradesh. Pp.108-48 in *In a Minority: Essays on Muslim women in India* (eds) Z. Hasan & R. Menon. New Delhi and New Jersey: Oxford University Press and Rutgers University Press.

—. Forthcoming-a. The First madrasa. Learned mawlawīs and the Educated Mother. *Islamic Education, Diversity and National Identity* (ed.) J.-P. Hartung. New Delhi: Sage.

—. Forthcoming-b. Investing in the Future: Education in the social and cultural reproduction of north Indian Muslims. *The Future of Muslims in India* (ed.) M. Hasan. New Delhi: HarperCollins.

Jeffery, P. M., R. Jeffery & A. Lyon. 1989. *Labour Pains and Labour Power: Women and Childbearing in India*. London: Zed Books.

—. 2002. Contaminating states: midwifery, childbearing and the state in rural north India. Pp.90-108 in *The daughters of*

Hariti: childbirth and female healers in south and southeast Asia (eds) S. Rozario & G. Samuel. London and New York: Routledge.

Jeffery, R. 1988. *The Politics of Health in India*. Berkeley: University of California Press.

Jeffery, R. & A. Basu (Eds) 1996. *Girls' Schooling, Women's Autonomy and Fertility Change in South Asia*. New Delhi: Sage.

Jeffery, R. & P.M. Jeffery. 1993a. Traditional Birth Attendants in Rural North India: the Social Organization of Childbearing. Pp.7-31 in *Knowledge Power and Practice: The Anthropology of Medicine and Everyday Life* (eds) S. Lindenbaum & M. Lock. Berkeley: University of California Press.

—. 1993b. A Woman Belongs to Her Husband: Female Autonomy, Women's Work and Childbearing in Bijnor. Pp.66-114 in *Gender and Political Economy: Explorations of South Asian Systems* (ed.) A. Clark. Delhi: Oxford University Press.

—. 1994b. The Bijnor Riots, October 1990: Collapse of A Mythical Special Relationship? *Economic and Political Weekly* 29, 10: 551-58.

—. 1997. *Population, Gender and Politics: Demographic Change in Rural North India*. Cambridge: Cambridge University Press.

—. 2000. Religion and Fertility in India. *Economic and Political Weekly* 35, 35-36: 3253-59.

—. 2005. Saffron Demography, Common Wisdom, Aspirations and Uneven Governmentalities. *Economic and Political Weekly* 40, 5: 447-53.

Jeffery, R., P.M. Jeffery & C. Jeffrey. 2005b. Social inequalities and the privatisation of secondary schooling in north India. Pp.41-61 in *Educational Regimes in Contemporary India: Essays on education in a changing global context* (eds) R. Chopra & P. Jeffery. New Delhi: Sage.

—. 2006. Patterns and Discourses of the Privatisation of Secondary Schooling in Bijnor, UP. *Education in South Asia* (eds) K. Kumar & J. Oesterheld. New Delhi: Orient Longman.

Jenkins, R. 1996. *Social Identity*. London: Routledge.

John, R.M. & R. Mutatkar. 2005. Statewise Estimates of Poverty among Religious Groups in India. *Economic and Political Weekly* 40, 13: 1337-45.

Jones, K.W. 1981. Religious Identity and the Indian Census. *The Census in British India: New Perspectives* (Ed.) N.G. Barrier. Delhi: Manohar.

Joshi, A.P., M.D. Srinivas & J.K. Bajaj. 2003. *Religious Demography of India*. Chennai: Centre for Policy Studies.

Kabeer, N. 1991. The Quest for National Identity: Women, Islam and the State in Bangladesh. Pp.115-43 in *Women, Islam and the State* (ed.) D. Kandiyoti. London: Macmillan.

—. 1999. Resources, Agency, Achievements: Reflection on the Measurement of Women's Empowerment. *Development and Change* 30, 4: 435-464.

Kakar, S. 1995. *The Colours of Violence*. New Delhi: Viking.

Kandiyoti, D. 1988. Bargaining With Patriarchy. *Gender and Society* 2, 3: 274-90.

— (ed.) 1991. *Women, Islam and the State*. London: Macmillan.

—. 1998. Gender, Power and Contestation: 'Rethinking Bargaining With Patriarchy'. Pp.135-151 in *Feminist Visions of Development: Gender Analysis and Policy* (Eds) C. Jackson & R. Pearson. London: Routledge.

Kapur, R. & B. Cossman. 1995. Communalising Gender/Engendering Community: Women, Legal Discourse and the Saffron Agenda. Pp.82-120 in *Women and the Hindu Right* (eds) T. Sarkar & U. Butalia. New Delhi: Kali for Women.

—. 1996. *Subversive Sites: Feminist Engagements with Law in India*. New Delhi: Sage.

Kasturi, L. 1996. Development, Patriarchy, and Politics: Indian Women in the Political Process, 1947-1992. Pp.99-144 in *Patriarchy and Economic Development: Women's Position at the end of the Twentieth Century* (ed.) V.M. Moghadam. Oxford: Clarendon Press.

Khan, M.E. 1979. *Family Planning Among Muslims in India: A Study of the Reproductive Behavior of Muslims in an Urban Setting*. Delhi: Manohar.

Khan, M.F. 1991. *Human Fertility in Northern India*. Delhi: Manak Publications.

Khilnani, S. 1997. *The idea of India*. London: Hamish Hamilton.

King, C.R. 1994. *One Language, Two Scripts: The Hindi Movement in Nineteenth Century North India*. Delhi: Oxford University Press.

Kingdon, G. & M. Muzammil. 2001. A Political Economy of Education in India. *Economic and Political Weekly* XXXVI, 32 & 33: 3052-62 & 3178-85.

Kingdon, G.G. & M. Muzammil. 2003. *The political economy of education in India: teacher politics in Uttar Pradesh*. New Delhi: Oxford University Press.

Kishor, S. 1993. "May God Give Sons To All": Gender and Child Mortality in India. *American Sociological Review* 58, 2: 247-65.

Kishwar, M. 1986. Pro Women or Anti Muslim? *Manushi* 6, 2: 4-13.

—. 1994. Codified Hindu Law: Myth and Reality. *Economic and Political Weekly* 29, 33: 2145-61.

Kohli, A. 1987. *The State and Poverty in India*. Cambridge: Cambridge University Press.

Kolenda, P. 1987a. Living the Levirate. Pp.45-67 in *Dimensions of Social Life* (ed.) P. Hockings. Berlin: de Gruyter.

—. 1987b. *Regional Differences in Family Structure in India*. Jaipur: Rawat Publications.

Kozlowski, G.C. 1989. Muslim women and the control of property in North India. Pp.114-132 in *Women in Colonial India: Essays on Survival, Work and the State* (ed.) J. Krishnamurthy. Delhi: Oxford University Press.

Knodel, J., R.S. Gray, P. Sriwatchin & S. Peracca. 1999. Religion and Reproduction: Muslims in Buddhist Thailand. *Population Studies* 53, 2: 149-164.

Krishnaji, N. & K.S. James. 2005. Religion and Fertility: A Comment. *Economic and Political Weekly* 40, 5: 455-58.

Krishnakumar, A. 1991. Canards on Muslims: Calling the Bluff on Communal Propaganda. *Frontline* 8, 15: 93-98.

Kumar, R. 1993. *The History of Doing: an Illustrated Account of Movements for Women's Rights and Feminism in India, 1800-1990*. New Delhi: Kali for Women.

Lal, M. 1999. Purdah as Pathology: Medical Research and Reproductive Health in 20th-Century India. Paper Presented to the SOAS Conference on Population, Birth Control and Reproductive Health in Late Colonial India, London, UK, 1999.

Latifi, D. 1999. Preserving Urdu through Self-help. *Economic and Political Weekly* 34, 22: 1321-1323.

Lerche, J. 2003. Hamlet, Village and Region: Caste and Class Differences between Low-Caste Mobilization in East and West UP. Pp.181-98 in *Social and Political Change in Uttar Pradesh* (eds) R. Jeffery & J. Lerche. New Delhi: Manohar.

Lelyveld, D.S. 1993. The Fate of Hindustani: Colonial Knowledge and the Project of a National Language. Pp.189-214 in *Orientalism and the Postcolonial Predicament: Perspectives on South Asia* (eds) C.A. Breckenridge & P. van der Veer. Philadelphia: University of Pennsylvania Press.

Levin, A., B. Caldwell & Barkat-E-Khuda. 1999. The Effect of Price and Access On Contraceptive Use. *Social Science and Medicine* 49, 1: 1-15.

Ludden, D. 1993. Orientalist Empiricism: Transformations of Colonial Knowledge. Pp.250-278 in *Orientalism and the Postcolonial Predicament: Perspectives on South Asia* (eds) C.A. Breckenridge & P. van der Veer. Philadelphia: University of Pennsylvania Press.

— (Ed.) 1996. *Contesting the Nation: Religion, Community, and the Politics of Democracy in India.* Philadelphia: University of Pennsylvania Press (Also Published As "Making India Hindu" By Oxford University Press).

Mandelbaum, D.G. 1974. *Human Fertility in India: Social Components and Policy Perspectives.* Berkeley: University of California Press.

—. 1986. Sex Roles and Gender Relations in North India. *Economic and Political Weekly* XXI, 1999-2004.

—. 1988. *Women's Seclusion and Men's Honor.* Tucson: University of Arizona Press.

Mani, L. 1989. Contentious Traditions: The Debate on Sati in Colonial India. Pp.88-126 in *Recasting Women: Essays in Colonial History* (eds) K. Sangari & S. Vaid. New Delhi: Kali for Women.

—. 1990. Multiple Mediations: Feminist Scholarship in The Age of Multinational Reception. *Feminist Review* 35, 24-41.

Mann, E.A. 1992. *Boundaries and Identities: Muslims, Work and Status in Aligarh.* New Delhi: Sage.

—. 1994. Education, Money and the Role of Women in Maintaining Minority Identity. Pp.130-68 in *Forging Identities: Gender, Communities and the State* (ed.) Z. Hasan. New Delhi: Kali for Women.

McNicoll, G. 1994. *Institutional Analysis of Fertility.* The Population Council Research Division Working Papers 62.

Mazumdar, S. 1992. Women, Culture and Politics: Engendering the Hindu Nation. *South Asia Bulletin* 12, 2: 1-24.

—. 1995. Women on the March: Right-wing Mobilization in Contemporary India. *Feminist Review* 49, 1-28.

Menski, W. 2001. *Modern Indian Family Law*. Richmond, Surrey: Curzon Press.

Metcalf, B.D. 1990. *Perfecting Women: Maulana Ashraf `Ali Thanawi's Bihishti Zewar A Partial Translation with Commentary* (trans.) B.D. Metcalf. Berkeley: University of California Press.

— . 1999. Women and Men in a Contemporary Pietist Movement: The Case of the Tablighi Jama`at. Pp.107-121 in *Resisting the Sacred and the Secular: Women and Politicized Religion in South Asia* (eds) P. Jeffery & A. Basu. New Delhi: Kali for Women.

Miller, B.D. 1981. *The Endangered Sex: Neglect of Female Children in Rural North India*. Ithaca: Cornell University Press.

Minault, G. 1994. Other Voices, Other Rooms: the View from the Zenana. Pp.108-24 in *Women as Subjects: South Asian Histories* (ed.) N. Kumar. Calcutta: Stree.

— . 1998. *Secluded Scholars: Women's Education and Muslim Social Reform in Colonial India*. New Delhi: Oxford University Press.

Mishra, S. 2005. Public Health Scenario in India. Pp.62-83 in *India Development Report 2004-05* (eds) K.S. Parikh & R. Radhakrishna. Mumbai: Indira Gandhi Institute of Development Research.

Mitra, S. & A. Fischer. 2002. Sacred Laws and the Secular State: An Analytical Narrative of the Controversy over Personal Laws in India. *India Review* 1, 3: 99-130.

Mody, N.B. 1987. The Press in India: The Shah Bano Judgment and Its Aftermath. *Asian Survey* 27, 8: 935-53.

Moghadam, V.M. (ed.) 1994a. *Gender and National Identity: Women and Politics in Muslim Societies*. London: Zed Books.

— (ed.) 1994b. *Identity Politics and Women: Cultural Reassertions and Feminisms in International Perspective*. Boulder: Westview Press.

Molyneux, M. 1998. Analysing women's movements. Pp.65-88 in *Feminist Visions of Development: Gender analysis and policy* (eds) C. Jackson & R. Pearson. London: Routledge.

Mooij, J. & M. Dev. 2004. Patterns of social sector expenditures: pre- and post-reform period. Pp.96-111 in *India Development Report 2004* (ed.) R. Radhakrishna. New Delhi: Oxford University Presss.

Moser, C. 1989. Gender Planning in the Third World: Meeting Practical and Strategic Gender Needs. *World Development* 17, 1: 1799-1825.

Moulasha, K. & G.R. Rao. 1999. Religion-Specific Differentials in Fertility and Family Planning. *Economic and Political Weekly* 34, 42: 3047-3051.

Mukhopadhyay, C.C. & S. Seymour (eds) 1994. *Women, Education and Family Structure in India*. Boulder: Westview.

Mukhopadhyay, M. 1994. Between Community and State: The Question of Women's Rights and Personal Laws. Pp.108-129 in *Forging Identities: Gender, Communities and the State* (ed.) Z. Hasan. New Delhi: Kali for Women.

—. 1998. *Legally Dispossessed: Gender, Identity and the Process of Law*. Calcutta: Stree.

Mumtaz, K. 1994. Identity Politics and Women: 'Fundamentalism' and Women in Pakistan. Pp.228-42 in *Identity Politics and Women: Cultural Reassertions and Feminisms in International Perspective* (ed.) V.M. Moghadam. Boulder: Westview Press.

Mumtaz, K. & F. Shaheed. 1987. *Women of Pakistan: Two Steps Forward, One Step Back?* London: Zed Books.

Murthi, M., A.-C. Guio & J. Drèze. 1996. Mortality, Fertility and Gender Bias in India. Pp.357-406 in *Indian Development: Selected Regional Perspectives* (Eds) J. Drèze & A. Sen. Delhi: Oxford University Press.

Narayana, G. & J.F. Kantner. 1992. *Doing the Needful: The Dilemma of India's Population Policy.* Boulder: Westview Press.

National Committee On The Status of Women. 1975. *Status of Women in India: A Synopsis of the Report of the National Committee (1971-74).* The Indian Council of Social Science Research/Allied Publishers.

Navlakha, G. 1994. Triple Talaq: Posturing at Women's Expense. *Economic and Political Weekly* 29, 21: 1264.

Obermeyer, C.M. 1992. Islam, Women and Politics: The Demography of The Arab Countries. *Population and Development Review* 18, 1: 33-60.

—. 1994. Religious Doctrine, State Ideology and Reproductive Options in Islam. Pp.59-75 in *Power and Decision: The Social Control of Reproduction* (Eds) G. Sen & R.C. Snow. Boston: Harvard School of Public Health.

Oesterheld, J. 2006. National Education as a Community Issue: The Muslim Response to the Wardha Scheme. *Education and Social Change in South Asia* (eds) K. Kumar & J. Oesterheld. New Delhi: Orient Longman.

Omran, A.R. 1992. *Family Planning in the Legacy of Islam.* London & New York: Routledge.

Omvedt, G. 1993. *Reinventing Revolution: New Social Movements and the Socialist Tradition in India.* Armonk & London: M. E. Sharpe.

Orsini, F. 2002. *The Hindi Public Sphere 1920-1940: Language and Literature in the Age of Nationalism*. New Delhi: Oxford University Press.

Osella, F. & C. Osella. 2000. The return of King Mahabali: the politics of morality in Kerala. Pp.137-162 in *The Everyday State and Society in Modern India* (eds) C. Fuller & V. Bénéï. New Delhi: Social Science Press.

Pai, S. 2002. Politics of Language: Decline of Urdu in Uttar Pradesh. *Economic and Political Weekly* 37, 27: 2705-2708.

Pai Panandikar, V.A. & P.K. Umashankar. 1994. Fertility Control and Politics in India. *The New Politics of Reproduction* (Eds) J.L. Finkle & A.A. Mcintosh. New York: Oxford University Press.

Palriwala, R. & I. Agnihotri. 1996. Tradition, the Family, and the State: Politics of the Contemporary Women's Movement. Pp.503-532 in *Region, Religion, Caste, Gender and Culture in Contemporary India* (ed.) T.V. Sathyamurthy. Delhi: Oxford University Press.

Pandey, A., M.K. Choe, N.Y. Luther, D. Sahu & J. Chand. 1998. *Infant and Child Mortality in India* (NHFS Subject Reports, No. 11). Mumbai and Honolulu: International Institute for Population Sciences and East-West Center.

Pandey, G. 1990. *The Construction of Communalism in Colonial North India*. Delhi: Oxford University Press.

—. 1991. Hindus and Others: The Militant Hindu Construction. *Economic and Political Weekly* 26, 2997-3009.

—. 1993. *Hindus and Others: The Question of Identity in India Today*. Delhi: Viking.

Papanek, H. 1979. Family Status Production: the 'Work' and 'Non-work' of women. *Signs* 4, 4: 775-81.

—. 1982. Purdah: Separate Worlds and Symbolic Shelter. Pp.3-53 in *Separate Worlds: Studies of Purdah in South Asia* (Eds) H. Papanek & G. Minault. Delhi: Chanakya Publications.

Parashar, A. 1992. *Women and Family Law Reform in India: Uniform Civil Code and Gender Equality*. New Delhi: Sage Publications.

—. 1997. Family Law as a Means of Ensuring Gender Justice for Indian Women. *Indian Journal of Gender Studies* 4, 2: 199-229.

Pathak, Z. & R.S. Rajan. 1989. "Shahbano". *Signs* 14, 3: 558-82.

Popkin, S. 1980. The Rational Peasant: The Political Economy of Peasant Society. *Theory and Society* 9, 3: 411-71.

Prakash, I. 1979. *They Count Their Gains--We Calculate Our Losses*. New Delhi: Akhil Bharat Hindu Mahasabha.

Qadeer, I., K. Sen & K.R. Nayar. 2001. *Public Health and the Poverty of Reforms: The South Asian Predicament*. New Delhi and Thousand Oaks CA: Sage.

Radwan, I. 2004. *Private Health Services for the Poor: Policy Note*. Washington DC: World Bank.

Rafat, Z. 2003. Muslim women's divorce and remarriage in a town of western Uttar Pradesh. Pp.75-99 in *Divorce and remarriage among Muslims in India* (ed.) I. Ahmad. New Delhi: Manohar.

Raheja, G.G. 1988. *The Poison in the Gift*. Chicago: University of Chicago Press.

—. 1995. "Crying When She's Born, and Crying When She Goes Away": Marriage and the Idiom of the Gift in Pahansu Song Performance. Pp.19-59 in >*From the Margins of Hindu Marriage: Essays on Gender, Religion and Culture* (eds) L. Harlan & P. Courtright. New York: Oxford University Press.

Raheja, G.G. & A.G. Gold. 1994. *Listen to the Heron's Words: Reimagining Gender and Kinship in North India*. Berkeley: University of California Press.

Rai, B. n.d. *Explosion of Muslim Population of India*. Chandigarh: B. S. Publishers.

Rajan, R.S. 2003. *The scandal of the state: women, law, and citizenship in postcolonial India*. New Delhi: Permanent Black.

Rajan, S.I. 2005. District level Fertility Estimates for Hindus and Muslims. *Economic and Political Weekly* 40, 5: 437-46.

Ramachandran, V. 2003. *Gender and Social Equity in Primary Education*. New Delhi: Sage.

Ramesh, B.M. & D. Retherford. 1996. *Contraceptive Use in India 1992-93*. International Institute For Population Studies NFHS Subject Reports 2.

Rao, M. 1999. *Disinvesting in Health: The World Bank's prescriptions for health*. New Delhi and Thousand Oaks, CA: Sage.

Reddy, P.H. 2003. Religion, Population Growth, Fertility and Family Planning Practice in India. *Economic and Political Weekly* 28, 33: 3500-09.

Registrar General India. 1976. *Fertility Differentials in India*. New Delhi: Ministry of Home Affairs, Government of India.

—. 1981. *Survey of Infant and Child Mortality, 1979*. New Delhi: Ministry of Home Affairs, Government of India.

—. 1982. *Levels, Trends and Differentials in Fertility 1979*. New Delhi: Vital Statistics Division, Office of the Registrar General India, Ministry of Home Affairs.

Registrar General & Census Commissioner, India. 2002. *Population, population in the age group 0-6 and literates by residence and sex- India and States/Union territories*. New Delhi: Ministry of Home Affairs.

—. 2004. Presentation on Religion. http://www.censusindia.net/religiondata/presentation_on_religion.pdf. Last accessed on 27 July 2005

—. 2005. SRS Bulletin Volume 39 No. 1. http://www.censusindia.net/vs/srs/bulletins/SRS_Bulletin_April_2005.pdf. Last accessed on 29 July 2005

Rex, J. 1986. *Race and Ethnicity*. Milton Keynes: Open University Press.

Rose, K. 1992. *Where Women are Leaders: The SEWA Movement in India*. New Delhi: Vistaar Publications, and London: Zed Books.

Russell, R. 1999a. Some Notes on Hindi and Urdu. Pp.131-137 in *How not to write the History of Urdu Literature and Other Essays on Urdu and Islam* (ed.) R. Russell. Delhi: Oxford University Press.

—. 1999b. Urdu in India since Independence. *Economic and Political Weekly* 34, 1 & 2: 44-48.

Saberwal, S. & M. Hasan. 1984. Moradabad Riots 1980: Causes and Meanings. *Economic and Political Weekly* 19, 3: 208-27.

Said, E.W. 1978. *Orientalism: Western Conceptions of The Orient*. New York: Pantheon.

—. 1993. *Culture and Imperialism*. London: Chatto and Windus.

Sangari, K. 1995. Politics of Diversity: Religious Communities and Multiple Patriarchies. *Economic and Political Weekly* 30, 51-52: 3287-3307, 3381-3389.

Sarkar, S. 1993. The Fascism of the Sangh Parivar. *Economic and Political Weekly* 28, 5: 163-167.

Sarkar, T. 1991. The Woman as Communal Subject: Rashtrasevika Samiti and the Ramjanmabhoomi Movement. *Economic and Political Weekly* 26, 35: 2057-65.

—. 1993. Rhetoric Against the Age of Consent: Resisting Colonial Reason and the Death of a Child Wife. *Economic and Political Weekly* 28, 36: 1869-1878.

Sarkar, T. & U. Butalia (eds) 1995. *Women and the Hindu Right*. New Delhi and London: Kali for Women and Zed Books.

Savage, D.W. 1997. Missionaries and the Development of A Colonial Ideology of Female Education in India. *Gender and History* 9, 2: 201-221.

Scott, J. 1985. *Weapons of the Weak: Everyday Forms of Peasant Resistance*. New Haven: Yale University Press.

Sen, A. 1990. Gender and Co-Operative Conflicts. Pp.123-149 in *Persistent Inequalities: Women and World Development* (Ed.) I. Tinker. New York: Oxford University Press.

Sen, I. 1990. *A Space within the Struggle: Women's Participation in People's Movements*. New Delhi: Kali for Women.

Shariff, A. 1995. Socio-Economic and Demographic Differentials between Hindus and Muslims in India. *Economic and Political Weekly* 30, 46: 2947-2953.

Sharma, U. 1980. *Women, Work and Property in North West India*. London: Tavistock.

—. 1986. *Women's Work, Class and the Urban Household*. London: Tavistock.

Sikand, Y. 2001a. Countering Fundamentalism: Beyond the Ban on SIMI. *Economic and Political Weekly* 36, 37: 3803.

—. 2001b. Targeting Muslim Religious Schools. *Economic and Political Weekly* 36, 35: 3342-43.

Singh, A. 1992. *Women in Muslim Personal Law*. Jaipur: Rawat Publications.

Singh, A.K. 2001. *Uttar Pradesh Development Report 2000*. Lucknow: New Royal Book Company.

Sridhar, V. 1991. Fiction and Fact: The Real Plight of the Minorities. *Frontline* 8, 15: 99-101.

Sunder Rajan, R. 2003. *The scandal of the state: women, law and citizenship in postcolonial India*. New Delhi: Permanent Black.

Szreter, S., H. Sholkamy & A. Dharmalingam. 2005. Contextualising Categories: Towards a Critical Reflexive Demography. Pp.3-32 in (eds) S. Szreter, H. Sholkamy & A. Dharmalingam. Oxford: Oxford University Press.

The Probe Team. 1999. *Public Report on Basic Education in India*. New Delhi: Oxford University Press.

United Nations. 1998. *Too Young to Die: Genes or Gender?* (ST/ESA/SER.A/155). New York: UN Department of Economic and Social Affairs, Population Division.

van der Veer, P. 1994. *Religious Nationalism: Hindus and Muslims in India*. Berkeley: University of California Press.

Vanaik, A. 1990. *The Painful Transition: Bourgeois Democracy in India*. London: Verso Books.

—. 1997. *The Furies of Indian Communalism: Religion, Modernity and Secularization*. London: Verso.

Varadarajan, S. (ed.) 2002. *Gujarat: the making of a tragedy*. New Delhi: Penguin Books India.

Vatuk, S. 1990. "To be a Burden on Others": Dependency Anxiety among the Elderly in India. Pp.64-88 in *Divine Passions: The Social Construction of Emotion in India* (ed.) O.T. Lynch. Delhi: Oxford University Press.

—. 1995. The Indian Woman in Later Life. Pp.289-306 in *Women's Health in India: Risk and Vulnerability* (eds) M. Das Gupta, L.C. Chen & T.N. Krishnan. Bombay: Oxford University Press.

Venkatachaliah, M.N. 1999. Language and Politics: Status of Urdu in India. *Economic and Political Weekly* 34, 26: 1659-1660.

Verghese, B.G. 2003. Misconceived and Mischievous. *The Week* 27 July.

Véron, R., S. Corbridge, G. Williams & M. Srivastava. 2003. The Everyday State and Political Society in Eastern India: Structuring Access to the Employment Assurance Scheme. *Journal of Development Studies* 39, 5: 1-28.

Visaria, P., A. Gumber & L. Visaria. 1993. Literacy and Primary Education in India, 1980-81 to 1991. *Journal of Educational Planning and Administration* 7, 1.

Wadley, S.S. 1994. *Struggling with Destiny in Karimpur, 1925-1984*. Berkeley: University of California Press.

—. 1995a. No Longer a Wife: Widows in Rural North India. Pp.90-118 in *From the Margins of Hindu Marriage: Essays on Gender, Religion and Culture* (eds) L. Harlan & P. Courtright. New York: Oxford University Press.

—. 1995b. The "Village Indira": A Brahman Widow and Political Action in Rural North India. Pp.225-250 in *Women in India: Two Perspectives* (eds) D. Jacobson & S.S. Wadley. Delhi: Manohar.

Working Group on Women's Rights. 1996. Reversing the Option: Civil Codes and Personal Laws. *Economic and Political Weekly* 31, 20: 1180-83.

World Bank. 1997. *Primary Education in India* (Development in Practice). Washington DC: World Bank.

World Health Organisation. 2005. *The World Health Report 2005*. Geneva: WHO.

Wright, T.P.J. 1983. The Ethnic Numbers Game in India: Hindu-Muslim Conflicts over Conversion, Family Planning, Migration and the Census. Pp. 405-427 in *Culture, Ethnicity and Identity* (Ed.) W.C. Mccready. New York: Academic Press.

Yuval-Davis, N. 1997. *Gender and Nation*. London: Sage.